WALKING IN ANDALUCIA

The Best Walks in
Southern Spain's Natural Parks

Guy Hunter-Watts

Walking in Andalucía is published by:

Ediciones Santana S.L.,

Apartado 422, 29640 Fuengirola (Málaga), Spain.

Tel 952 485 838. Fax 952 485 367.

E-mail santana@net.es

First published in November 2000.
Revised Editions February 2002, March 2003.
Copyright © Guy Hunter-Watts.

Photography by the author
Cover photograph courtesy of Stap Reizen
Photograph of author courtesy of John Brough

Design and typesetting by John Harper.

We would like to express our thanks to the Servicio Geográfico del Ejército. All of the maps reproduced in this guide are based on their L Series, Scale 1:50000. See our introduction for details of where to order all maps listed.

No part of this book may be reproduced or transmitted in any form or by any means without the prior permission in writing from the publishers.

Imprime Gráficas San Pancracio S.L.,

Polígono Industrial San Luis,

Calle Orotava 17, Málaga, Spain.

Depósito Legal: MA-1.233/2000   ISBN 84-89954-24-0

ACKNOWLEDGEMENTS

My first thanks must go to the many people who helped when I was researching this guide. In the Alpujarras, José and Inge of Sierra y Mar in Ferreirola were incredibly generous with their time and their local knowledge. When I was walking in Aracena, Sam and Jeannie Chesterton provided me with a wonderful base at Finca Buen Vino. In La Axarquía, Sandra Costello of Casa La Piedra in Cómpeta was exceptionally kind in sharing some of her favourite routes with me. In the Gaucín area, Tiger and Melanie of Unseen Andalucía and Patrick Elvin, a man who knows the mountains around Gaucín like few others, pointed me in the right direction and even found time to accompany me on some of the walks. And when I was on the point of losing my way to Genalguacil, Sarah and Anthony Wheatley put me on the right path. Your help has been invaluable.

Finally, I would also like to thank the many readers who have written to tell me about changes they have encountered on these routes and an extra thankyou to Alan Peacegood who has become my second set of eyes and feet in Andalucía. ¡Mil gracias a todos!

About the Author

Guy Hunter-Watts has lived in a small village in the mountains close to Ronda since 1989. He worked as a trekking guide in the Andes and the Indian Himalaya before settling in Spain. He now combines work as a walking guide with researching travel guides and running a small B&B.

Contents

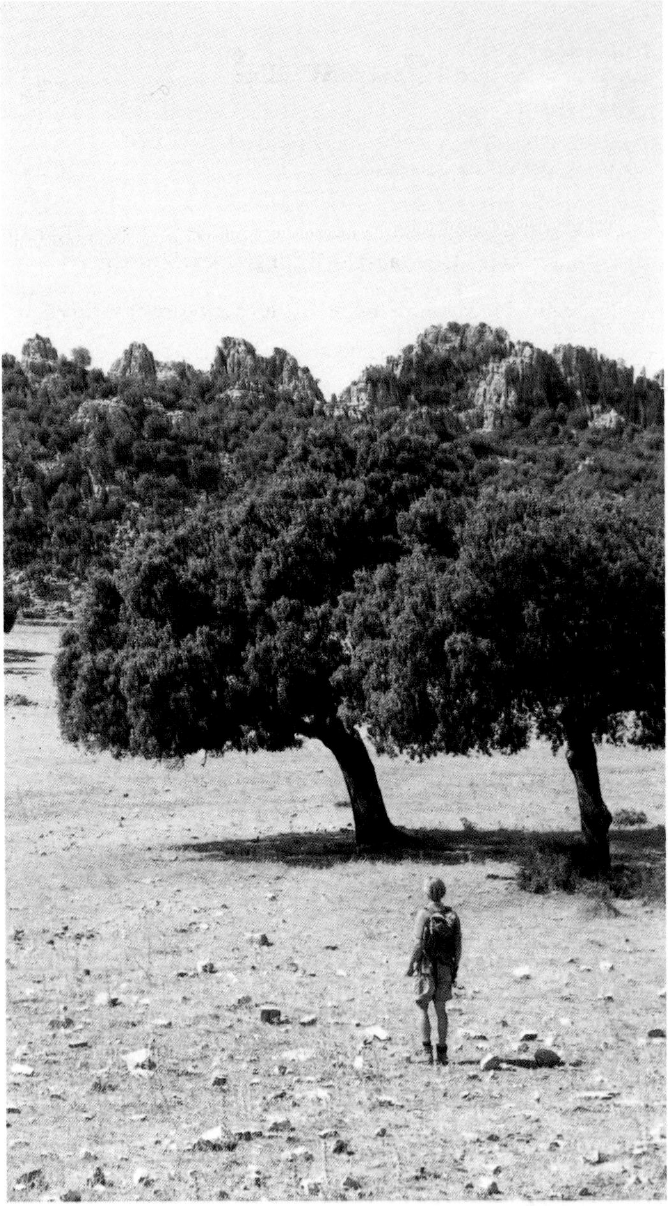

Foreword

"That something exists outside ourselves and our preoccupations, so near, so readily available, is our greatest blessing".

"There are things we will never see, unless we walk to them".

"Walking is egalitarian and democratic; we do not become experts at walking and one side of the road is as good as another".

—Thomas A. Clark on Walking.

My first experience of inland Spain came at the age of twenty one when I rode an old sit-up-and-beg bike across inland Andalucía from Huelva in the West to Murcía in the East. What most excited me were the vast, open spaces through which I was travelling. Coming from southern England the small number of cars and the sparsely populated landscape seemed as exotic a sight as the palm trees and bougainvillea which gave nearly every remote *cortijo* such a heady allure.

Many years later I returned. This time I exchanged two wheels for two leather boots and headed for the mountains south of Ronda. Again I was inspired and moved by the huge expanse of wild and rugged mountains. The landscape felt unbridled compared with the more domesticated country-side that I had left behind.

It is this sense of space which makes walking in Andalucía so special. More and more people are beginning to walk Spain's southern Sierras, yet the vast majority of the routes remain blissfully undiscovered. If you decide to head for the hills with this guide you can be sure of two things: you will be walking through areas of great natural beauty and will meet with few other walkers. There is nothing to detract from the sheer pleasure of simply going out for a walk.

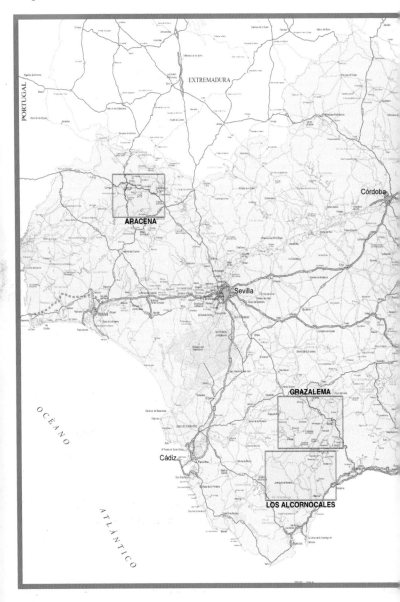

PORTUGAL

EXTREMADURA

Córdoba

ARACENA

Sevilla

OCÉANO

GRAZALEMA

Cádiz

ATLÁNTICO

LOS ALCORNOCALES

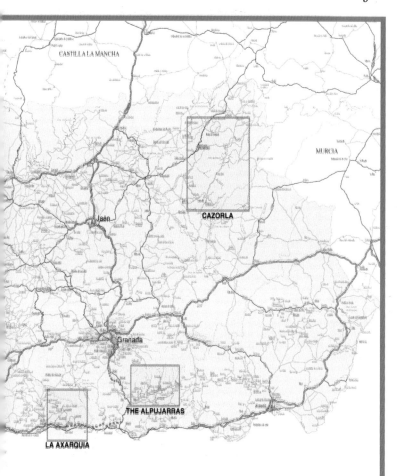

CASTILLA LA MANCHA

MURCIA

Jaén

CAZORLA

Granada

THE ALPUJARRAS

Almería

LA AXARQUIA

MAR MEDITERRÁNEO   Andalucía and the Natural Parks
described in this guide.

Introduction

The mountains and villages of Andalucía

Few people are aware that Spain, after Switzerland, is the most mountainous country in Europe or that the walking here can be as good as anywhere on the Continent. Perhaps it is because people have long associated holidays in Spain – especially in Andalucía – with sun and sea, cheap wine and paella. Inland Spain has always been a little too raw, too different, for the package tourists who prefer the familiarity and safety of their cosmopolitan, beachside hotels.

Yet the coastal belt represents just a tiny part of the incredibly rich fabric of Spain. If you travel just a few kilometres inland you will find any number of pretty villages where there is scarcely a foreign resident and where the idea of *pueblo* (it means both 'village' and 'people') remains as vibrant and as strong as it has for centuries. Not to visit these villages is, in a sense, not to visit Spain. Ask a Spaniard where she or he is from and rather than replying *"España"* they invariably give you the name of their home village. Ask one of Andalucía's many emigrant workers what they miss most and they will probably tell you that, after their family and friends, it is their annual village fiesta.

Many of these villages are wrapped into the fabric of the great belt of the Cordillera Bética mountains which run from east to west across Andalucía. This vast range includes Spain's highest peak, the Mulhacén which, in spite of its southerly position, will sometimes have snow on its upper reaches for nine months of the year. And within this mighty, rumpled chain of mountains there are no fewer than twenty Natural Parks, each of them – believe me – with a character all of its own.

The aim of this walking book is two-fold. It is not only to introduce you to the most beautiful of Andalucía's Natural Parks but also to lead you to their most attractive villages and small towns. To this end, all of the walks described here (with just a couple of exceptions) either link two villages or are circular routes departing and ending in villages **which are not only worth visiting but where there is good accommodation and food available**. Surely one of the greatest pleasures after a long walk is to tuck into a delicious meal – and then slump into a comfortable bed.

And the really good news is that over the last decade or so there has been a silent revolution in the hills of Southern Spain. The Spanish – and also their northern European visitors – have woken up to the beauty of the interior of the country. All of a sudden it has become fashionable to head for the hills rather than for the beach: 'turismo rural' has entered the vernacular. The most tangible result of all this has been a huge increase in the number of places to stay.

What is so positive about this trend is that it is fostering a new pride in traditional country life. Age-old handicrafts, cuisine, architecture, medicine and folklore are again being valued, and are even providing incomes for people who might otherwise have been obliged to work far from home. Hand in hand with this 'rediscovery' of the villages of inland Spain has come a new-found interest in the hills and mountains which surround them. Old paths are being cleared, routes are being marked out and groups of walkers, mostly from northern Europe, are beginning to arrive.

If you are looking for purpose-built trails of the sort that you find, say, in the Parks of the USA, then the walking in Andalucía will probably not be for you. Many of these walks follow old drovers' paths which have had scant use since the coming of the roads. They can be rough or loose underfoot, occasionally overgrown (we mention these parts in our text) and when waymarking exists, it can be confusing. But none of the walks described in this book will pit you against Nature. They are, I believe, all beautiful, all different, and all well within the capabilities of anyone who walks on a fairly regular basis.

When to walk in Andalucía

As a general rule the very best time to walk in Andalucía is from late April through to early June and from mid September to the end of October. You are almost guaranteed mild, sunny weather. It is warm enough to picnic and the chances of rain are slight. The wild flowers tend to be at their very best in late April/early May and this is the time when most walking companies tend to plan their walks.

The months that most walkers avoid are July and August. Temperatures are generally just too high to make walking easy or pleasant. If you limit yourself to shorter circuits, get going really early, and take plenty of water you can still enjoy walking in summer. But you should be in good physical shape.

If you are prepared to risk rain then the winter months can be a wonderful time to be out walking, especially from December to February when rainfall is generally less than in November, March and April. 'Generally' means exactly that: rainfall statistics for the past century confirm all of the above but the past decade, with the prolonged drought of the nineteen-nineties, followed by some unusually wet winters, provide no steady yardstick against which to base your predictions.

The exception to the above is the Cazorla Park which is further north than any of the other Parks included in this book. Here the Mediterranean influence is less marked and there may well be snow and ice on the higher routes from November onwards. On the other hand the Alpujarras, although higher than Cazorla, rarely have snow settling beneath 1200m and to walk with the snowy Sierra Nevada as a backdrop makes for truly memorable experience. But you will need to be well-equipped and ready for brusque changes in temperature.

The routes

I have tried in each Park to provide a mixture of half-day and full-day walks, which will

a) introduce you to the most attractive area of each Park

b) lead you to the most interesting villages of the area

The **introduction** to each walk should give you a feel for any given itinerary and the **walking notes and maps** will give you a good idea of the distance and the differences in height that you will encounter.

How to use the walking notes

The walking notes, together with the individual route map, should allow you to follow these walks without difficulty. But we recommend that you always have a compass and the recommended map of the area, in addition to the one that we provide in this book.

Distance: self-explanatory.

Rating: the walks are graded in three brackets:

- Easy – covers shorter itineraries where there is little climbing.

- Medium – rather longer walks with some steeper up/downhill sections.

- Difficult – denotes a longer route that has a number of steep up and downhill sections.

If you are reasonably fit and used to walking then you should experience no difficulty with any of these routes. For the 'difficult' routes the most important thing is to allow yourself plenty of time, and take plenty of water. The very longest of the walks described is 19km (12 miles). But remember: what can be an easy walk in cooler weather can become a much more difficult one in the heat. I have based my rating system on walking in cooler weather, of the sort that you are likely to encounter in Spring or Autumn in Andalucía.

Time required: The number of hours under 'time required' is our estimation of how long you should allow to really get the most out of a particular walk, allowing for rest stops and lunch breaks. **This is different to the bracketed timing of the actual itinerary:** this is my timing for walking each of the routes, without breaks, at an 'average' walking pace. If you find that your pace is much slower or faster than mine, don't worry: these timings are intended to give you an idea of how far into any particular walk you might be. You could simply ignore them: it will be pretty obvious from the map how far you have to go.

Map: recommends the best map to have with you on any particular walk. Sometimes I suggest an alternative, too.

Definition of terms: the notes are, I hope, easy to follow. When describing the walks, I've used "track" for any thoroughfare wide enough to permit vehicle access and "path" to describe one that is wide enough only for pedestrians and animals.

Routes can change!

I have tried to be as accurate as possible in describing the routes in this book. But paths, like roads, can change. We would be very grateful for your feedback on any changes that you have encountered so that we can pass them on to other readers.

Walking check list

The two most important things to remember when you walk in Andalucía are:

- A good supply of water. Carry a minimum of 1 litre and preferably 2 litres of water. During the warmer months the greatest danger facing you is heat exhaustion, so wear loose-fitting clothing, a hat, and drink lots of water.

- Comfortable, well broken-in walking boots. No walk is enjoyable with blisters.

You should also remember the following (this list is compiled with your maximum safety and comfort in mind):

- Water bottle (Swiss "Sigg" bottles are good.)

- Hat, Sun block, Sunglasses

- Map and Compass

- Swiss army knife (or similar)

- Torch, Whistle

- Mobile phone. (Mobile phone coverage inevitably gets worse in the mountains but if you have a mobile phone it would be silly not to take it along.)

- Waterproofs (according to season).

- Fleece or Jumper: remember temperatures can drop rapidly at the top of the higher passes.

- Picnic + rubbish bag

- First aid kit. To include standard items + antihistamine cream, plasters, plastic skin etc for blisters, insect repellent.

- Water purifying tablets

- Chaps. (Even if you don't use them back home, a pair of nylon or canvas gaiters/chaps could be worth taking along on some of these walks. There are many prickly plants in Andalucía and from June onwards the thistles can be vicious.)

- Walking stick. (More and more people are using light weight aluminium walking sticks: the best of them even have shock-absorbing tips. The evidence shows that these help reduce injuries and conserve energy.)

- Chocolate/Sweets or Glucose tablets

Things to remember when walking in Andalucía

- Close all gates. You will come across some extraordinary gate closing devices. They can take time, patience and effort to open and to close.

- *Ganado bravo*. Watch out for this sign because it designates an area where you could find bulls. None of the walks described here take you through these areas. A sign saying *coto* or *coto privado de caza* designates an area where hunting is permitted (in season) and does not mean that you are walking on private property. The *cotos* are normally marked by a small rectangular sign divided into a white and black triangle.

- **Fire**. In the dry months the hillsides of the South become a vast tinder-box. Be very careful if you smoke or use camping stoves.

- **Rubbish**. Take yours and - why not? – other people's back with you.

- **Springs**. Occasionally you will come across mountain springs on these walks. I have not mentioned them because in Andalucía you never know when they might dry up. Always check what is happening upstream before you drink: you might be just yards from livestock.

Maps

Under each of the general sections I have recommended the best maps available for the area. At the back of this book we have included a bilingual order form which we hope will make the whole process of ordering much easier from within Spain. All of the places listed will send maps *contra reembolso,* i.e. you pay when the maps are delivered to you by the postman.

In Andalucía the best place to order maps from is:
    L.T.C.
    Avenida Menéndez Pelayo 42-44,
    41003 Sevilla.
    Tel: 954 425 964 • Fax: 954 423 451.

In Málaga the best place for maps is:
    La Casa del Mapa.
    Panaderos 2, esq. Puerta del Mar. Málaga
    Tel: 952 061 421 Fax: 952 600 216.

In Granada the best place for maps is:
    Cartográfica del Sur. Valle Inclán 2.
    Tel: 958 204 901.

The staff are really friendly and they have a great range of guide books including some in English.

In Madrid the best map shop is:
    La Tienda Verde.
    Calle Maudes 23 & 38, 28003 Madrid.
    Tel: 915 330 791 • Fax: 915 336 454

(La tienda Verde also has the most comprehensive selection of guide books in the whole of Spain).

In the UK the best place for maps is:
    Stanfords
    12-14 Long Acre, London, WC1
    (Tel: 0207 836 1321 • Fax: 0207 836 0189).
They have catalogues listing the Spanish maps which they
stock and also operate a mail order service.
In the USA one of the better Map outlets is The Complete
Traveler Bookstore. In New York: Tel 212 6859 007 and in
San Francisco: Tel 415 923 1511.

Books

Ornithology
The classic field guide (small enough for your day pack) is:
A Field Guide to Great Britain & Europe.
Peterson, Mountfort & Hollom (ISBN 0-00-219900-9).

Birdwatching on Spain's Southern Coast

John R. Butler, Santana Books (ISBN 84-89954-20-8). This field guide also contains detailed maps of both coastal and mountain locations.

Botany

My favourite field guide for the flowers in the area is:

Wildflowers of Southern Spain.

Betty Molesworth Allen. (ISBN 84-88127-06-5). The book not only gives you the botanical information but also describes medicinal and culinary uses of the plants listed.

Also good, and a manageable size, is:

Wildflowers of the Mediterranean.

Burnie. (ISBN 0-75131011-5).

Accommodation

We have tried to include hotels, hostals and B&B-type places that are in the villages where walks begin or end. The places that we have included all have one thing in common: they are clean and welcoming.

Nearly all of them offer breakfast and most can prepare an evening meal. Some will even make you a picnic lunch if you let the owners know the night before. We suggest other good places to eat (under **Best Eats**) when there is no food available or when there is a particularly good restaurant close by.

The prices quoted are meant to be a guideline and you may get a lower price out of season. There may also have been slight increases. Check when you phone or fax to book. Remember, too, that some of the smaller places don't accept credit cards. And try to book ahead, especially at the weekend and during school holidays.

The hotels of Andalucía often make extensive use of marble, the perfect material for the searing heat of the summer. But in winter it means that floors can be icy cold. So a pair of slippers can be a godsend. Some cheaper hostals don't provide soap so always have a bar of your own along. And when travelling in the colder months, it is always a good idea, if you know your ETA, to ring ahead and remind owners to switch the heating on before your arrive.

Eating in Southern Spain

You should be aware when planning your excursions that the Spanish eat much later than is the custom in Britain and the USA. Lunch is often not generally available until around 2pm and few people sit down to dinner much before 9pm, so dining rooms rarely open before 8.30pm. Remember, too, that there is nearly always a *menu del día* available, even if it is automatically assumed that you will want to eat *à la carte*. They are often marvellous value. A common lament amongst walkers is that breakfast isn't served in some places until 9am, which can mean not getting going until nearly 10am. If you are keen to make an earlier start, take a thermos along. Most places will willingly fill it up with tea or coffee the night before and may even leave you breakfast.

Author's note

As anyone will know who walks regulary in the country, paths, like roads, can change: fencing can go up, new tracks can appear and waymarking can be added.

I would welcome any feedback from readers about any changes that you might have encountered to the routes described in this book so that these can be incorporated when this book next goes to print. I also welcome your suggestions as to other areas and walks that you think should be included in subsequent editions of this guide book.

Please write to Guy Hunter-Watts, El Tejar, 29430 Montecorto (Málaga) or e-mail me at eltejar@mercuryin.es

Many thanks.

ARACENA

The area.

The Natural Park of the Sierra de Aracena y Los Picos de Aroche lies an hour and a half by car to the north-west of Seville and encompasses an impressive 184,000 hectares of the province of Huelva. The range forms the western-most tip of the Sierra Morena, the mountainous belt which forms a natural divide between Spain's central Meseta and the Guadalquivir valley to the south. The sierra gradually loses height as it cuts sabre-like across Andalusia, with its last foothills reaching out and across the border into Portugal.

All of the walks described in this chapter lie within the Sierra of Aracena, one of the park's three mountain ranges, which stretches west from the delightful town of the same name. Within this Sierra are a string of attractive villages which, until just 50 years ago, were connected to one another by an elaborate network of drovers' paths. These century-old thoroughfares cut out from the villages by way of cultivated *huertas* (see glossary) where small groves of citrus alternate with carefully tended vegetable plots. Most walks described follow these old paths. In many places the original cobbling remains intact and there are long sections of path which run between old stone-walls, covered in mosses and lichens. There are few walkers, gradients are for the most part not too steep and the itineraries are generally easy to follow.

The area gets surprisingly heavy rainfall considering its southerly position: the Atlantic weather systems cross Portugal unhindered before being forced upwards by this last spur of the Iberian massif which rises to a height of nearly 1000 metres in little more than a dozen miles. In spite of the predominantly impervious subsoil, substantial ground cover ensures that much of this rainfall is retained. This fact, along with a relative absence of the use of pesticides, ensures that the wildflowers here are spectacular in all but the summer months.

The most singular feature of the area is the extensive *dehesa* system of woodland management (see glossary) whose persistence has ensured that a staggering 90% of the area of the Park remains forested. The trees most characteristic of the *dehesa* are evergreen and cork oaks. They provide rich and sustainable grazing for the much-prized Iberian pigs which are so much a feature of the Aracena hills: you'll see them scuttling away from you beneath the oaks on any of these walks. No trip to the Sierra would be complete without tasting the Jabugo ham, the region's most famous culinary delicacy.

The hillsides are also characterised by large swathes of chestnut groves. These became an important part of the local economy after being introduced in the period following the Reconquest. They have flourished in the unusually warm and damp conditions of the Sierra. The trees are at their most impressive in the autumn when the leaves are on the turn, whilst in winter their heavily coppiced forms look almost baobab-like when the leaves are down. To see them cloaked in winter mists is a sight never to be forgotten.

But the Park, particularly at its periphery, also encompasses extensive stands of eucalyptus and pine. Most of this forest mass owes its origin to the deforestation which followed the passing of the charcoal burners. When it came to replanting, indigenous species were abandoned in favour of those which could be quickly harvested. The routes in this book avoid these areas whenever possible: the impoverished subsoil provides little of interest as far as flora and fauna are concerned and in many places denuded hillsides have suffered severe erosion.

Although the scenery here is less wild or rugged than in other mountain ranges of the South – you are always aware that the hand of man has been instrumental in fashioning the landscape – there are few areas which offer more attractive walking than the Aracena Park. Both long and short-distance paths have recently been waymarked and the region is bound to attract a growing number of visitors. So visit as soon as possible.

If you plan to stay for a number of days be sure to stay at least one night in Aracena and then, perhaps, move on to Linares, Alájar, or Almonaster. All three villages have a beauty all of their own and are worth a second or third night. My personal favourite is Alájar. It has a wonderful small *posada,* and the extraordinary Peña de Arias Montero towers above the village.

Other Walks

Several waymarked routes criss-cross the park. The small guide *Los Senderos de la Sierra de Aracena y Picos de Aroche,* available from the Aracena tourist office, describes these routes, allbeit with very scant detail: don't attempt to follow the routes without a map. There is no English translation as yet. To the North of the N433 road leading from Aracena to Portugal are two parallel, long-distance paths: the GR41 and the GR48. Both cut east-west across the park.

The scenery is not as pretty as that of the centre of the Park
- and you are also skirting round the eucalyptus belt. The
GR41.3 runs too close to the N433 for my personal liking.
Much more attractive is the GR42.1 which cuts a lovely loop
out from Galaroza via Jabugo and Almonaster then on to
Aroche at the Western end of the Park.

Maps.

The best maps are the standard 1:50000 map of the Servicio
Geográfico del Ejército. 98% of walks described in this sec-
tion are covered by Sheet (hoja) Aracena (917). A tiny part
of the walk east from Aracena to Carboneras via
Corteconcepción spills over onto the Instituto Nacional
Geográfico map: Sheet (hoja) Santa Olalla del Cala (918).

Best Places to Sleep

Aracena

Hotel Sierra de Aracena.
Tel: 959 12 61 75.
Fax: 959 12 62 18.
Reliable and attractive mid-range hotel just a couple of minutes walk from the main square. No evening meals but you are close to several restaurants. Approx. 50 euros. (Taxis: Sr. González 608 54 89 93 or Vicente 959 12 84 29). **Best eats**: Restaurante José Vicente, Bar El Porvenir, Bar Manzano or Meson-Bar P'taca.

Alájar

La Posada.
Tel & Fax: 959 12 57 12.
A delightful small hotel just yards from the pretty main square. Simply decorated rooms and a tiny dining room where breakfasts and evening meals are served. Approx 45 euros. (Taxi: Angel 959 12 57 09 or 689 64 89 25). **Best Eats**: El Padrino (weekends) or El Molino.

Los Marines

(just to the north of Linares de la Sierra)

Finca Buen Vino.
Tel: 959 12 40 34
Fax: 959 50 10 29.
Without doubt my personal favourite, although more expensive than other places listed. Sam and Jeannie Chesterton are huge fun, know many of the walks, all the best restaurants and have created a supremely congenial house-party atmosphere at Buen Vino. Approx 200 euros including breakfast and dinner. (Taxi: Sam will arrange). **Best Eats**: here. Jeannie is Corden-Bleu trained (she runs cookery courses).

Almonaster la Real

Hostal La Cruz.
Tel: 959 14 31 35.
A simple hostal at the entrance of the village with no-frills accommodation and a popular restaurant beneath. Safe rather than memorable – but the village is delightful. Approx. 30 euros. (Taxi: Alfonso 959 14 31 30).
Best eats: Casa García.

Casa Garcia
Tel: 959 14 31 09.
An attractive small hotel at the entrance to the village which has recently been refurbished. Excellent food and outstandingly good value. Approx. 45 euros. (Taxi: Alfonso 959 14 31 30)
Best eats: Here

Aracena Circuit

Distance:	12 km.
Time Required:	4 / 4.5 hours
Rating:	Medium
Map:	1: 50000 Aracena (917)

The Walk of the Bountiful Dehesa

This is an excellent first half-day walk in the Aracena Sierra. Although the walk begins in the town centre, you very quickly leave traffic behind and the scenery is terrifically varied. Narrow cobbled paths passing by irrigated orchards, broader tracks lead through an attractive swathe of *dehesa* (glossary), the pretty village of Linares lies half way through the walk and some old farms along the way foster that longing for a rural retreat. Gradients are for the most part gentle, with just one section of steeper climbing **(about 20 minutes)** on the return leg.

The Route

The walk begins at Café Bar Manzano on Aracena's pretty main square.

Turn right out of the bar, cross the street and go past the Caja de San Fernando. At the end of this street turn right at the sign for *Gruta de la Maravillas*. Continue all the way down this street, passing by hotel Los Castaños, until you reach a square with several palm trees.

Here bear left along a one way street, passing by the old wash house to your left. At the end of the street, bear left again and just 75m later turn right at a sign *Conservas Jabugo*.

Pass the ticket booth of the football pitch and you come to a new housing development. Here keep left on a sandy track following white and yellow way-marking.

Soon the path runs between old dry-stone walls and drops gently down. Pass Hacienda Boca de Oro. The path, easy to follow, passes through an area of

dehesa (see glossary). Keep to main track until you reach a wire-and-post gate. Here swing sharp right and descend through gorse and oaks, now on a sandy path.

Soon you see a better defined path higher up to the left. Climb up onto this path then continue your descent, sticking to roughly the same course.

This broad path narrows and reaches a gate. Don't go through the gate but bear sharp right, drop down, cross a (dry) stream then swing to the left. Climb for a short distance with the stream down to your left. Soon you descend again and emerge onto a track which leads on in the same direction **(50 mins)**.

You meet with another track just as it hairpins up the hill. Turn left here, go down the hill and pass a pretty farmstead to the left of your track with a water tank.

At the gate that leads into the farm, bear right and you reach another gate (waymarked). Go through the gate and continue along the track. There is a wall to your left. Go through a second gate and climb upwards on a sandy track, passing a ruin to your right.

The path roller coasters and joins a better defined track. Here turn right and climb up between high walls. Stick to this track all the way to Linares (you are following the old drovers' path of *Las Deshadillas*, once one of the principal livestock routes of south-western Spain. Pass Casa El Saucejo to your right, cross a bridge and then after a fairly level section of track, drop down and cross a second bridge. Soon you will come to the outskirts of Linares **(1 hr 20 mins).**

Here the path skirts right and contours round the bottom of the village before coming to an ugly brick tower. Swing right up the hill - unless you are visiting the village in which case go straight on and later return to this point. Soon you come to a sign *Aracena 9.7kms*. Don't worry, your route is shorter. From here you have only 5.5kms to walk! Pick up a pretty section of cobbled track that soon becomes a track. It runs more or less parallel to the Aracena-Linares road that is above you to your left.

Pass a series of culti-vated terraces. The track narrows again to become a path. Eventually, you once again meet with a track. Continue on your same course and soon you'll pass a sign for Cortijo La Herreria, to your right. At the next fork swing right, drop down and cross the river.

Cross a second bridge, swing right and then climb, at first gently but soon more steeply (there are occasional concreted sections). Don't deviate from the main track. The path levels out and you reach a sign explaining what constitutes a *dehesa* **(2 hrs 15 mins).**

At the sign, go straight ahead (a track leads right and left), continuing along an attractive footpath.

Soon you pass a marker post. The path meets a narrow track. Continue on your same course, now descending through olives and cork oaks. The track widens, begins to climb, then swings sharp left towards the road.

Don't climb up to the road but rather branch right and continue along a track that runs parallel to the road. You descend along an attractive final section of track and the castle of Aracena comes into view. You reach the wide open area that you passed earlier in the walk, where a new housing development has been built **(2 hrs 50).**

Go along its top edge to the swimming pool, then continue along a street with a no-entry sign, passing the Feria ground on your right. You arrive once again at the palm-lined square you passed at the beginning of the walk. From here retrace your steps back to the main square **(3 hrs 15 mins).**

Distance:	10 km
Time Required:	4/4.5 hours
Rating:	Easy
Map:	1:50000 Aracena (917) & Santa Olalla del Calá (918)

Aracena to
Carboneras via
Corteconcepción

The Walk
of the Happy Pigs

This is an easy half day walk, much of it along beautiful old muleteer's paths. You first follow a fertile valley out from Aracena before climbing up through groves of olives and stands of cork oak beneath which you're bound to see grazing pigs grubbing for acorns. If you visit Corteconcepción, a half-hour diversion, you will need to double back on yourself- but only for a short distance. The descent to Carboneras is particularly attractive with long views east towards the Sierra del Norte. The variety of the terrain and abundance of fruit trees and hedgerows means there is a great variety of birdlife. The walk ends with a short, easily-arranged taxi ride back to Aracena.

The Route

The walk begins outside the Bar Manzano in Aracena's main square, the Plaza Marquesa de Aracena. From here head across the square to El Casino and climb up Calle Mesones past La Iglesia del Carmen. At the top of the street bear right and at the end of this next street turn sharp left and climb to the Ermita de San Roque. Keep to the left of the chapel, pass under a bridge then follow a quiet road downhill. After about 600m fork right onto a track: there is waymarking and a sign for Corteconcepción.

You arrive at a small shrine dedicated to the Virgin. Bear left here and drop down through olive and almond groves. You go past a number of farm-

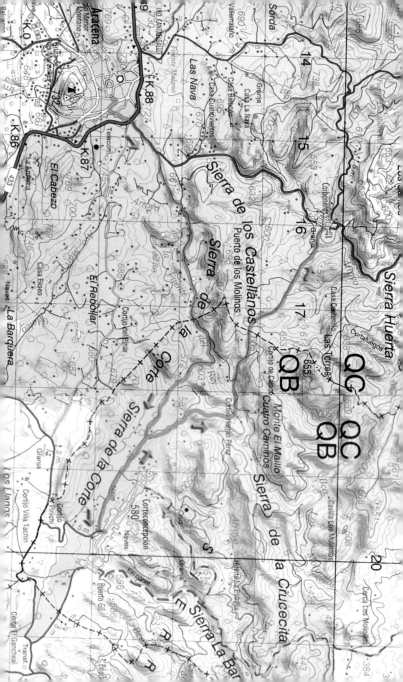

steads and then pass by La Fuente del Rey, just to one side of the track. The track swings up to the left and then descends again through more olive groves and passes the entrance of Finca La Postora.

Continue down through well-watered groves: agave, pomegranate and prickly pears lend an exotic hue. Shortly before you reach the river there is a modern white building to your right and here the track divides **(40 mins)**.

Bear right, descend, cross the (dry) river, and climb up past the white house. The track narrows to become a footpath which climbs steadily upwards. You come to a bench by a metal gate: the path bears right. There is white and yellow waymarking. Keep to the main path: every so often you see the old cobbling of the path. You pass a first green gate then just 10 metres after a second one and your path meets with two others, one branching left, the other right, the point known locally as Tres Caminos (**1 hr 15 mins**).

If visiting Corteconcepción, turn right and follow this path all the way to the village but remember that later you will need to return to this same point.

Shortly before the village, cross directly over the tarmac road leading from the village to Aracena then carry on along Calle Diputación to the centre of the village (**1 hr 30 mins**).

A good picnic spot could be beside the Church of Nuestra Señora de la Concepción at the very top of the village.

It has views out across the Aracena Reservoir.

After visiting the village, return to Tres Caminos mentioned above. Here, arriving from Corte-concepción, go straight on (don't bear left back along the path you came along earlier in the day). There is a sign *Carboneras 5 kms* (**2.00 hrs**).

Now follow a broad path that shortly divides. Branch right and go down past a farm. Drop past the yellow and ochre entrance gate of a farm and continue down to the river, passing by Los Molinos and a small pump house.

On the other side of the river, turn left and continue along the right bank of the Arroyo de la Fuente del Rey.

You reach a grove of eucalyptus trees and at its far end the track swings hard left. Here branch right (there is a marker post) and follow another track that climbs through a rather bleak swathe of land that is being re-planted. You'll see plastic tubing around the seed-lings, protection from foraging animals.

Careful! Just five min-utes from where you turned right at the euca-lyptus grove, just as you reach a rather more open area of hillside, you will see a large evergreen oak leaning down the hill towards you. Here branch left off the track onto a small, indistinct path that soon becomes better defined as it climbs up between two fences. You should once again see waymarking.

Once over the top of the pass, you drop steeply down a very pretty path (some sections are cobbled). You pass by a drinking trough and continue to descend between two stone walls and shortly meet with a track.

Here continue on your same course, now climbing. Look for pigs beneath the oaks. Continue on this track and you will shortly see Carboneras beneath you to your right.

You now descend, cross a (dry) stream and climb up a well-paved track to the village, entering it via Calle La Pasa (**3 hrs 20 mins**).

From here you could pick up a waymarked route which leads back to Aracena at the top of the village. But I don't recommend this route: it takes you through a sad swathe of eucalyptus trees, has some steep climbing and I was once set upon by more than a dozen dogs whilst their shepherd-owner looked on!

Much better to end this walk with a beer in one of the village bars and ring for a taxi to bring you back to Aracena (see page 27). The church, with its unusual red campanile, could be a good place to rendezvous with your driver.

Distance:	11 km
Time Required:	4/4.5 hours
Rating:	Medium
Map:	1:50000 Aracena (917)

Alájar Circuit

The Walk of the Forgotten Hamlet

This is one of the loveliest walks in the Sierra. It links two exceptionally pretty villages, the walk is easy to follow and there is only one steep climb. The long sections of cobbled path, the abandoned hamlet of Los Madroñeros and the peacefulness of the walk all contribute to make this a very favourite excursion. It is a walk to be savoured and is best combined with a leisurely picnic beneath one of the old oaks or olives which you pass by before reaching Linares de la Sierra. Or you could eat at the Mesón Arrieros in Linares.

The Route

The walk begins in the main square of Alájar. At the bottom of the square head up Calle San Bartolomé passing the Caja de San Fernando to your left. When you reach a church turn left into Calle San Marcos. The road soon bears right, passes the small Plaza de Miguel Moya then drops down Calle Pintor Antonio Milla past the restaurant Casa El Padrino. At the end of the street you climb slightly and will see a sign for Sendero Aldea de los Madroñeros. At this sign turn left and climb up a steep track that is at first concreted. Soon you are descending between old stone walls and there are cobbled sections of path. There are wonderful views to the south. This is an exceptionally beautiful beginning to the walk. Soon you see the small hamlet of Los Madroñeros up ahead (**30 mins**).

You come to a sign. It tells that in the mid 19th century, the hamlet had a

population of 150 but that it is now *deshabitado*, apart from the last Sunday in the month of August when a pilgrimage takes place in honour of Nuestra Señora de la Salud Venerada. The path drops steeply down to the hamlet. Once you reach the first houses bear left, away from the church, to reach a large grass-covered central square.

Go directly across this open area, pass between two houses, and you'll pick up a path that leads between beautiful old walls, taking you away from the hamlet. You should pick up waymarking. Cross a (dry) stream and the path winds on between evergreen and cork oaks. Look for grubbing pigs. The path reaches a gate **(45 mins)**.

Go through the gate and climb gently upwards. Pass by Cortijo Mailozana and soon your path descends and crosses the poplar-lined course of the Barranco de los Madroñeros. Then continue along a pretty cobbled

path. Somewhere around here would make a nice picnic/elevenses spot. The path, sandier now, passes an old ivy-covered palm tree, bears left and passes behind a farm.

You wind past old olive groves and grubbing pigs and shortly Linares comes into sight, down below you to your left. Go through a wire-and-post gate and the path narrows once again. You wind down on a final steep, cobbled section of path, cross a stream via a footbridge and then loop to the outskirts of the village that you enter just beside a small hotel **(1 hr 30mins)**.

Make sure to climb up and visit the village which is one of the prettiest in the Sierra. Then retrace your footsteps back to the hotel and here bear sharp to the right, then immediately left, and follow a narrow path that runs between high walls and has citrus groves on either side. You reach a wooden gate. Bear right and when you come to a fork bear right again, and climb to

reach a cobbled track
where you turn left. You
should see a sign here:
Alájar 8.9 km.

You pass the village
cemetery and soon will
have the oleander-filled
stream to your left. Con-
tinue along this track, pass
a picnic site (avoid a
steeper track that branches
right here) and prepare
yourself for a long, steep
climb.

The countryside opens
out and you occasionally
see the road up above you,
to the right. The track
narrows, becomes a path
and continues to climb
upwards, cobbled at times.
Eventually you meet the
Alájar-Linares road **(2 hrs
30 mins)**.

Here you turn left and,
after just 20 yards, turn
left again and descend
sharply on a track which is
paved for the first few
yards. After just 100 yards,
at a fork in front of a blue
metal gate, go left. There is
a signpost that points the
way to Alájar.

Drop down a path that at
first hugs the left bank of
the stream before crossing
over to its right bank.

Soon the path reverts to
track and continues de-
scending until it reaches
the first houses of Alájar,
where it meets with the
road. Bear left here and
wind down Calle Rafael
Montesinos. At the end of
the street, bear left again
by a telephone, continue
along Calle Virgen de la
Salud, then bear right in
front of the Casa de
Padrino.

Follow the wall of the
church of San Marco along
and then turn to the right
and drop down past the
Caja de San Fernando back
to the main square of
Alájar **(3 hrs 15 mins)**.

Alájar Circuit

Distance:	17 km
Time Required:	6.5/7 hours
Rating:	Medium/Difficult
Map:	1:50000 Aracena (917)

The Walk
of the Sensible Hippy

This longish walk links three of the very prettiest of the Sierra's villages. It is a tremendously varied excursion. It takes you through groves of olive and cork oak, pine forest and *dehesa* (see glossary), and you constantly switch between narrow paths and farm tracks. The first section of the walk is a little more difficult to follow than some of the walks listed here. But you pass several farms, so help is at hand should you take a wrong turn. And later you pick up waymarking. An exquisite final section of cobbled path leads you back to Alájar, a fitting reward for the steep climb up through the pines between Santa Ana and Castaño del Robledo. The path is occasionally rough underfoot, especially on the final section of the walk.

The Route

The walk begins in the pretty main square of Alájar in front of the *ayuntamiento*. At the bottom of the square, turn right into Calle Médico Emilio González, then turn left at hotel La Posada and go down Calle Constitución. Take the first right into Calle Talero, then take the first turning to your left.

You soon reach a fork. Bear right and descend on a cobbled path that runs between stone walls. The path widens to become a track and soon merges with a much broader track where there is a sign – *Stop 150m*. Bear right for just 100 yards, then turn left and descend steeply on a narrow path through a stand of cork oaks. You arrive at a fork by a gate with barbed wire. Here go

right. You are now climbing slightly. The track soon forks once again. Take the left option and soon you will pass a gate marked *Año 1984*. You descend, cross a stream, then climb and reach a farm house with a fountain. Here bear right and you arrive at the tiny hamlet of El Cabezuelo.

At the end of the hamlet, after passing a tiny *humilladero* (glossary), don't bear right up towards the road but rather swing sharp left down a narrow, slightly overgrown path. Soon the path climbs again and comes up to meet with the road. There is a pretty drinking fountain. Go left here and follow a wall along, passing a house with a water tank. Your path soon meets with a track. Go straight across here and the path again drops downhill. When you reach another track bear left, go down the hill and pass through the yard of a farm **(35mins)**.

Continue descending. There is *dehesa* to your left

and right. You cross a (dry) stream, bear right and follow a pretty section of track that runs between high walls. You begin to see waymarking – white and yellow stripes. The track becomes less distinct, climbs slightly away from the wall to your left but keeps roughly parallel to it. A few lone pines look rather incongruous amongst the cork oaks.

The track leads up towards a sign – *coto privado de caza*. Here bear slightly right, then swing left onto a path that runs parallel to a wall to your left. After about 150 yards, pick up a narrow path that runs closer to the wall on the same course. Look for the marker post.

Soon you have a metal-posted fence to your right. Where this fence ends, the path bears slightly right and climbs before it swings left and merges with a track that drops down the hill. You are in an area of transition between *dehesa* and pines. There are occasional signs for *coto*.

The path forks and up ahead to the left you'll see a red sign on a tree. Here turn right, pass under the branches of a low-growing oak, drop down and cross a (dry) stream. Another very pretty section of the walk leads you on between stone walls, past a huge cork oak. The path again drops down and you follow stepping stones across the (dry) river of La Ribera de Santa Ana La Real **(1 hr)**.

Climb slightly, pass by some low farm buildings to your left. Here keep to your same course, straight on up the hill. Don't swing hard round to your right! Soon you'll see waymarking. You pass a *calera* (lime pit) to your right, then a pigsty to the left. The track widens, descends and once again narrows to become a path, that at times runs next to a water channel.

You wind uphill between old cork oaks. Some sections of the path are cobbled. Soon it widens and becomes a cobbled track and you reach the first *huertas* (small patches of cultivated land) of the village. Don't take a first temping path that branches up right - it leads to the hamlet of La Presa - but continue on the same cobbled track. It soon bears right and leads you up into Santa Ana La Real. You pass a fountain, climb up calle Constitución into the village **(1 hr 30 mins)**.

You should visit the pretty main square, Plaza de España, and maybe Bar La Mezquita for refreshments. Otherwise, carry on up to the top of the village and turn right onto the Alájar road, passing the Colegio Público Arco Iris. After about 1 km, directly opposite a sign on the right for La Presa, swing left onto a path that climbs up to the top of the ridge **(1 hr 40 mins)**.

You then descend and soon the path leads along the left hand side of a grove of chestnuts. Shortly afterwards you will have a wall to your right. At the end of the wall, turn right (be sure not to go straight

on) and descend to the valley floor. You'll see a farm up ahead and shortly the track divides. Branch left, cross over a wooden bridge and climb for about 100 metres to a point where the track once again divides. Branch right and climb up into the pines on a rather eroded (and steep) section of bulldozed track. You could take the left fork up to the waterfall called Los Chorros de Hoyarancón, a good place for a picnic (it would take you half an hour to get up and down).

Just 100 metres or so after the fork, watch for waymarking to the right. You should now follow this track all the way to the top of a first ridge **(2 hrs 15 mins)**.

Here bear left and cross through an area where there has been a forest fire. The pine forest begins to thicken. You pass a sign for Castaño. You are following a line of pylons, climbing again. The path eventually levels and then descends until you arrive at the cemetery of Castaño del Robledo. The track leads past a pretty chapel to your left **(3 hrs)**.

Swing right up into the village. You reach a small square with a fountain where you bear right into Calle Real, then right again and climb Calle José Sánchez Calvo to reach the church and the main square.

From here go up Calle Arias Montero and, shortly before the street levels, opposite no.11, turn right and pick up a path that brings you to a wooden marker post. Here swing left onto a lovely cobbled path, quite overgrown in parts. It eventually merges with a track and leads up through chestnut groves to the top of a rise. Here descend for just 150 metres to a marker post.

Careful! Don't swing left and upwards but rather continue straight on down on your same course, following a well-defined track that leads through stands of chestnut, pine and cork oak.

The track narrows, follows a (dry) stream bed along and becomes more difficult underfoot. But it soon improves and you are once again on a lovely path with walls to either side. Pass through a wire-and-post fence and then a second one. The path becomes cobbled again and continues on down. It is quite overgrown in parts. You meet a wider track (**4 hrs**).

Here you bear left. Soon the track narrows again and you'll see a branch going off to the right. Ignore it and carry straight on. Once again, the track broadens and you zigzag down and past the Ermita de la Virgen de Los Angeles.

You come to an area of irrigated terraces and pass by a pretty hamlet with a friendly bunch of hippy inhabitants. It's easy to see why they should have chosen this delectable spot.

The cobbled path drops down, passes by a spring, then bears right and reaches a track which leads down to meet with the road. Head straight across and soon you will be back in the village square (**4 hrs 30 mins**).

Almonaster Circuit

Distance:	9 km
Time Required:	4/4.5 hours
Rating:	Medium
Map:	1:50000 Aracena (917)

The Walk
of Patience and Humility

Although this walk is much shorter than some of those described in this chapter, it is a surprisingly varied half-day walk. Your point of departure, Almonaster, is one of the Sierra's most attractive villages and the paths you follow on this walk must be as pretty as any in the Sierra. The reward for the steep climb up from Arroyo is a gorgeous final section of path that loops steeply down to the village. Don't be put off by the two short sections of tarmac road. There are a few prickly plants on the more overgrown parts of this walk but it is still doable in shorts.

The Route

The walk begins in the pretty main square of Almonaster la Real in front of the *ayuntamiento*.

Cross the square towards the tobacconist and drop down Calle El Pino. At the bottom, swing right into Calle Cristo and climb gently up towards the road leading to Cortegana.

Go past the ham factory, then take a cobbled path which leads in front of the chapel dedicated to Nuestra Señora de la Humildad y Paciencia. The path bears right and meets the road by a builder's yard. Follow the tarmac for a short distance, passing the *butano* yard and the cemetery. You pass by a pretty farm called El Prao to the left of the road.

Just 50 metres past El Prao, turn left off the road onto a track. It drops down past a marker post and narrows to become a cobbled path. You'll see waymarking – red and white, GR (*gran recorrido*)

and yellow and white, PR (*pequeño recorrido*). Pass a newly built farm on the left and continue descending.

You cross a (dry) stream where the path winds right and climbs for a short distance.

The path widens and shortly reverts to track. Soon it runs between fences to either side. You pass two ugly green gates – to the left and the right of the track - and continue downhill. Again the path narrows, bears sharply to the right, becomes cobbled again and then descends and crosses a (dry) stream **(45 mins)**.

Just as you climb up from the stream, turn sharp right. Don't go straight on! You now pick up marker posts again. You are climbing with the stream down to your right. You dog leg at the top of a rise and come to a railway line. Cross the track and climb on the same course. The path soon becomes better defined and once again it becomes cobbled.

You reach the outskirts of the hamlet of Los Acebuches. Go up the main street through the village, pass by a phone box and you come up to a junction. Turn right here, follow the road for about 500m and where pylons cross overhead, turn right off the road onto a narrow path. At the first fork in the path go left, cross a (dry) stream and climb.

The path, cobbled in parts, leads up to the tiny hamlet of Arroyo, where you take the first street to the left and climb steeply up to the road above the hamlet. Turn right here, and soon you'll meet the road from Cortegana to Almonaster, where you turn right, down the hill.

Pass a bus stop and you will see a modern house to the left of the road. Just past this house, bear left onto a cobbled path. It climbs steeply up through an area of small, cultivated *huertas*. You have a climb of about 200m ahead of you, more or less parallel to the left bank of a tributary of the Acebuches stream that you crossed earlier in the walk.

Climb up past an old water tank and soon cork oaks give way to pines. Eventually you come to an old farm building to the left of your path. It has an animal byre built from old railway sleepers. Just past it, you reach a fork. Branch left and continue climbing steeply upwards. The path narrows, becomes more overgrown, and passes by a chestnut grove. The countryside opens out and you reach the top of the 783 metre-high pass **(1hr 45 mins)**.

Continue on your same course, now descending gently, and you will meet with a sandy track. Turn right here. Ignore a marker post that points you left. Pass through a chestnut grove and soon a fence runs to the left of the track. Continue on down.

Shortly you go through a gate and the path becomes more indistinct, but there are marker posts. Pass by

another farm that you leave well over to your left, then come to a tumbledown wall. Here the path, rather indistinct now, bears slightly right, keeping the wall just to its left.

Soon it becomes easier to follow and leads you through a wire-and-post gate and along the edge of a field (keep the bed of the stream to your left - don't turn up to the right). After a short distance the path swings left, passes through a gap in the hedge and picks up a better-defined, cobbled path that runs down the hill, sticking close to the bank of the stream.

Another path comes in from the left to meet with yours. Here bear right and carry on down. A metal fence now runs to the left of the path. You pass through a wire-and-post gate and will see olive groves to your left.

The path, still descending, describes a series of beautiful loops, then meets a track where you turn

right. Soon you will come to a fork. Go left here and pick up another cobbled section of path. This was part of the old drovers' route that lead all the way to Mérida!

You are now dropping down towards Almonaster, and there are fine views of the old Mezquita. Just before your path reaches the river, bear right past an old flour mill (a sign explains the workings). Continue along this cobbled path, pass by a second flour mill with a palm tree and you will come to the road leading from Almonaster to Alájar.

Pass under the road through a tunnel and follow a beautiful narrow path to the village. Here you pass a phone box and Restaurante La Cruz and then, at the end of a square, follow Calle Francisco Montero up the hill. At the top of the street, turn left, pass bar Almonaster and then the *farmacia*, and you arrive back in the main square of the village **(2 hrs 45 mins)**.

GRAZALEMA

The area

The Grazalema Natural Park straddles the provinces of Cádiz and Málaga and encompasses the most south-westerly mountain range in Europe – the very tail-end of the Cordillera Bética. This rugged massif, predominantly composed of limestone and dolomite, rises dramatically up from the rolling farmlands around Jérez to a height of nearly 2000 metres. Although the park is comparatively small compared to others in Andalusia – it covers an area of just over 500 square kilometres – its terrain is extraordinarily varied. Jagged formations of karst give way to poplar-lined valleys, thick stands of cork and evergreen oaks alternate with old groves of olives and almonds and with fields of wheat and barley. The scenery changes with every turn in the path and the wildflowers here are as good as anywhere in Europe.

The extraordinary botanical variety – you will find more than a third of the Spain's plants within this small area – is the result of unusually complex climatic conditions. Continental, Mediterranean and Atlantic influences are all present and the village of Grazalema, plum in the centre of the park, receives more rainfall per square inch than anywhere in Spain. It is a remarkable micro climate. Villages just five miles from Grazalema receive a quarter of the rainfall. But don't let this put you off coming to walk. The rainfall is markedly seasonal – November, April and May tend to be the wettest months – and at other times of the year the chances are the weather will be good. This abundant rainfall means that the area is remarkably green by Andalusian standards and explains the existence of the large stand of pinsapo pines (*abies pinsapo Boiss*) on the northern slopes of the Sierra del Pinar.

The Park is an ornithological wonderland. You are bound to see hoopoes, wheatears, oriol, warblers, shrikes, rock thrushes, choughs and a whole lot more besides. But most notable are the raptors. Eagles (booted, short-toed and

golden) are easily spotted, and it is not unusual to see 100 or more griffon vultures on the wing. The largest colony in Europe inhabits the rocky ledges of the Garganta Verde close to Zahara de la Sierra (there are exceptional views of the gorge on the Benamahoma-Zahara walk). Here, as in other parts of Spain, numbers are being maintained thanks to various feeding sites in the high Sierra. One of the major migratory roots between Europe and Africa runs along the western fringe of the park.

What makes the park a double treat are not only the walks but also the pueblos blancos or white villages. All the walks described in this book begin in one of them. These villages – nearly all of them of Moorish origin – contain some of Spain's most distinctive "popular" architecture. Narrow streets of whitewashed houses, most of them with wrought iron rejas (window grills), drop steeply down the hillsides. Often just walking from the bottom to the top of a village is a hike in itself. The mountain perches are testimony to these villages having been built with defence in mind. This was the area of the ever-changing frontier or *frontera* between Moslem and Christian Spain.

Grazalema, plum at the centre of the park and one of the very prettiest villages in the area, has long been a popular destination for walking groups from the UK and also with the Spanish from Sevilla and Cádiz who flock in at the weekends. So book ahead unless you are staying out of season, on a weekday. Better still, stay in one of the quieter villages at the edge of the Park like Zahara, Montecorto, Benaocáz or Montejaque.

Other Walks

El Pinsapar. The classic Grazalema itinerary takes you through the heart of the Pinsapo forest. This full-day excursion begins on the road leading from Grazalema to Zahara. After a stiff climb of nearly 1000 feet, a broad path leads through a large stand of pinsapos, one of the few remaining stands of these exceptionally beautiful pine trees (*abies pinsapo Boiss*). You need a permit to do the walk. You can get from the Park offices in Grazalema or El Bosque. Get going early to avoid school parties and other groups.

Routes around Grazalema

There are two recently waymarked routes – both half days – that begin near the campsite on the road above the village. A good and easy-to-follow day's walk is to follow the river Campobuche (sometimes called the Gaduares) to Montejaque and then return by taxi. It is also easy to follow the route from Grazalema to Zahara that drops down the Gaidovar valley, skirts round Monte Prieto to Arroyomolinos, where a track begins and leads you nearly all the way to Zahara.

Benaoján to Ronda. Details of this half-day walk can be obtained from the Molino del Santo in Benaoján Estación (see accommodation). It follows the old drovers' path and the final approach to Ronda, via a narrow gorge, is magnificent.

Accompanied walks. The owner of El Tejar, the author this guide, (see accommodation) leads guided walks in the area and has route notes for many other local walks. He can even provide you with a dog to take on your rambles.

Maps

The best map of the area is the 1:50000 mapa/guía of the Junta de Andalucía/Instituto Geográfico Nacional. You can normally find it at the Grazalema newsagents and the two Park Offices (El Bosque and Grazalema). The map covers all 6 itineraries listed here. Next best alternative are the standard I.G.N.1:50000 maps. Sheets (hojas) Ubrique 1050, Olvera 1036, Cortes de la Frontera 1064.

Best Places to Sleep

Benaoján Estación

Hotel Molino del Santo.
Tel: 952 16 71 51
Fax: 952 16 73 27.

Pleasant river-side hotel popular with Brits. Plenty of local knowledge and help with route planning from Andy Chapell, the owner, who is a keen ornithologist. Vegetarian food available. Approx. 80-130 euros. (Taxi: Pepe. 952 16 71 94). **Best Eats**: here.

Montecorto

El Tejar.

Tel & Fax: 952 18 40 53.
Managed by Guy Hunter-Watts, author of this guide, this is the best place from which to explore the park. Picnics can be prepared and the owner has his own hand drawn maps of many walks in the area. Great views, great value. Approx. 60 euros. (Taxi: Antonio 952 184 118). **Best Eats**: here.

Montejaque

Palacete de Mañara.

Tel: 952 16 72 52
Fax: 952 16 74 08.
Recently opened in an attractive position, on the main square of Montejaque – which can be noisy. Approx. 55 euros. (Taxi: Paco 952 16 72 18) **Best Eats**: tapas here or next door in Bar Alemán.

Near to Ronda

Hotel La Fuente de la Higuera

Tel: 952 114 355
Fax: 952 224 356
A short drive from some of the routes described here. A stylishly converted olive mill in the hills just outside Ronda. Prices from 100 – 150 euros + IVA (Taxi: Luis Fuentes 649 362 437). **Best Eats:** Here or just around the corner at Venta El Polvorilla (sic).

Grazalema

Casa de Las Piedras.

Tel & Fax: 956 13 20 14.
Pleasant family run hotel at the heart of Grazalema. Both food and rooms are good value. A no-frills place, bedrooms have tiny shower rooms but are clean and comfort-able. The hotel can organise horse trekking with the Al-Hazán stables (Tel 956 23 42 35 or 610 32 91 46). Approx. 45 euros. (Taxi: Rafael 956 13 20 14) **Best Eats**: here or restaurante Cádiz el Chico.

El Bosque

Hotel Las Truchas.

Tel: 956 71 60 61
Fax: 956 71 60 86.
Just a short drive from the begin-ning of the Benamahoma-El Bosque walk at western end of the park. Pleasant river-side hotel with spacious rooms and good food. Approx. 55 euros. (Taxi: Oracio 956 71 61 99) **Best Eats**: here.

Zahara

Hotel Marqués de Zahara.

Tel & Fax: 956 12 30 61.
Small family-run hotel at the heart of the village. Rooms vary in size and can be noisy. Service occasionally sullen. Approx 50 euros. (Taxi: Diego 956 12 31 09 or Antonio 956 12 31 42). **Best eats**: tapas at Los Estribos or Bar Vicente.

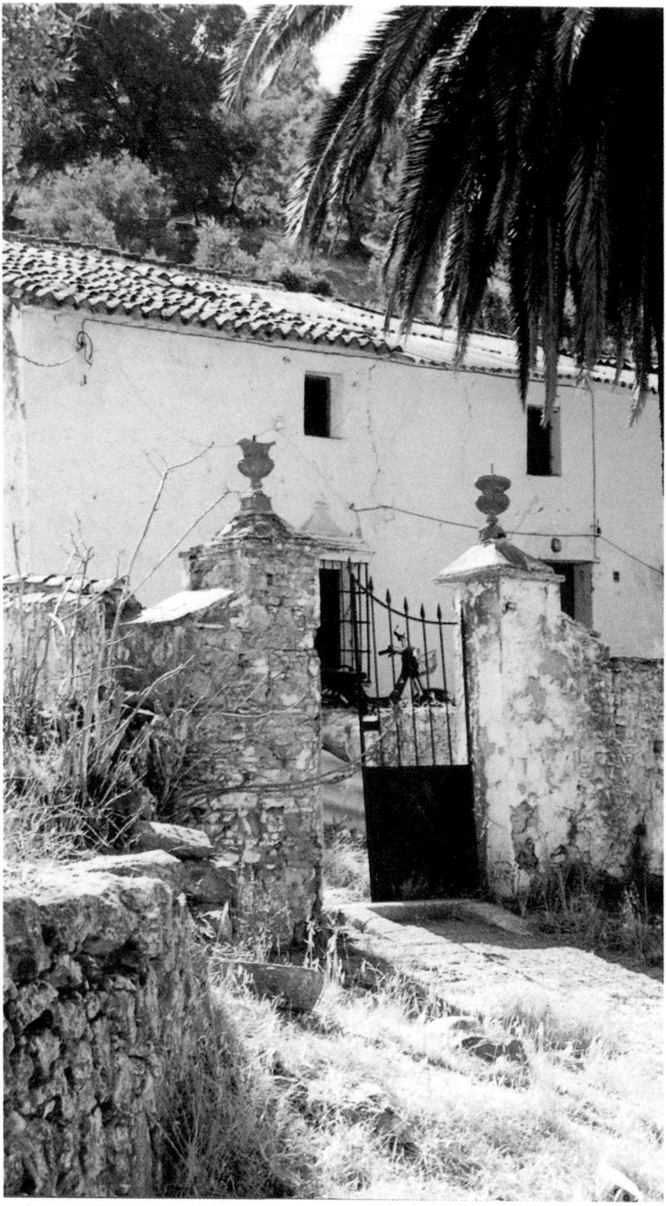

Distance:	9kms
Time Required:	2/2.5 hours
Rating:	Easy
Maps:	1:50000 Parque Natural Sierra de Grazalema or 1:50000 1050 Ubrique & 1064 Cortes de la Frontera

From Benaoján Estación to Jimera de Líbar

The Walk of Mr. Henderson's Railway

This short and easy walk follows a delightful riverside path which links the sleepy village of Benaoján Estación with the sleepier-still hamlet of Jimera de Líbar Estación. It begins at the Molino del Santo, a hotel and restaurant just up from railway line. What makes it such a lovely half-day walk is that you can set off after a late breakfast, dawdle along the way, have a long lazy lunch in the excellent Quercus restaurant in Jimera de Líbar Estación, then return by train to the Molino or to your car (departure from Jimera is at 4.48pm, arriving at Benaoján Estación at 4.56pm but always check because of slight seasonal variations). If this idea appeals, begin this walk at about 11am. You could turn this into a longer walk by retracing your footsteps back along the Guadalete valley from Jimera.

The Route

The walk begins at the Molino del Santo in Benaoján Estación. Turn left out of the Molino's main entrance and walk down the hill until you reach a stop sign at a level crossing. Turn left along the railway line, cross over a river and at a second level crossing turn right and cross over the railway track.

The road drops down, crosses the river Guadiaro and leads up to a sign marking the beginning of the walk that recommends you allow (a very generous) four hours. Turn right off the road at the sign and follow a track that soon passes by an abandoned

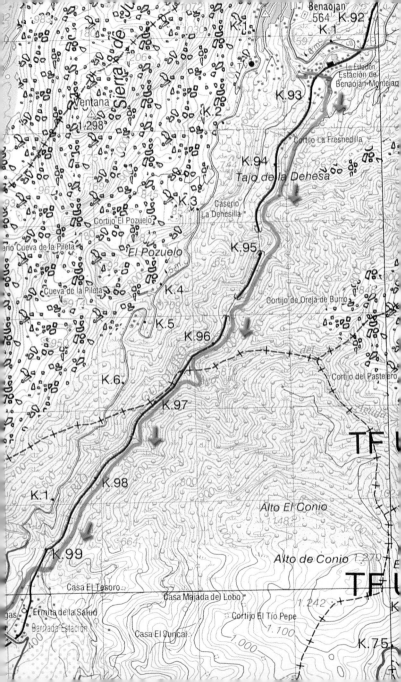

farm with three magnificent palm trees. The railway and the river are now to your right.

I always think of Mr Henderson on this walk, the British engineer responsible for the construction of the Ronda-Algeciras line. The train that plied this route came to be known as the Smugglers Express. It went so slowly that contraband butter, cocoa and tobacco from Gibraltar could be sold from the train windows!

The track narrows to become a path which crosses a small wooden bridge then bears right and passes a ruined farm.

After this farm, the path divides. You should take the left fork and climb slightly away from the river before it descends once again to the river. Soon the railway runs on your side of the river. Carry on along this same path. You eventually drop down, cross a (dry) stream and a little further on a concrete water channel

runs to the left of your path (**1 hr 10 mins**).

Continue along the path, pass a rusting black and white sign 'Ojo al tren' and you reach a sign 'Via Pecuaria'. Here loop sharply to the right, cross the railway track then bear left and follow a narrow path between a fence on the left and brambles on the right. The path soon meets a dirt track which in turn shortly meets with a concrete road. Here turn left and you come to the Quercus restaurant in a converted railway shed. From here the station of Jimera de Libar is just 100m along the railway track (**1 hr 35 mins**).

After lunch either return by this same route or take the train. It is just a ten minute ride back to Benaoján Estación along Mr Henderson's railway line.

Distance:	17km
Time Required:	8/9 hours
Rating:	Medium/Difficult
Map:	1:50000 Parque Natural Sierra de Grazalema or 1:50000 1050 Ubrique & 1064 Cortes de la Frontera

The Walk
of the Líbar Valley

This is another of the great walks of the Grazalema Park. The Líbar valley has a beauty all its own. Its flat bottom makes for easy walking, yet the mountains to either side are wild and rugged. This long walk is easy to follow and like the Montejaque circuit takes you far away from civilisation. Once you drop into the valley, you'll only come across half a dozen farms in almost five hours! Although you are following a driveable track for much of the walk, it is rare to meet with farm vehicles. But there is a mountain hut about half way along the valley that attracts other walkers at weekends, so try to do this walk on a weekday. Because you have quite some distance to cover, try to get going fairly early with a picnic and plenty of water and be prepared for a steep climb up from Cortes first thing. (As this book went to press, the route was about to be waymarked on the new GR route).

The Route

The walk begins in front of Cortes de la Frontera's town hall. With the town hall behind you, turn right and go along the main street passing the Unicaja bank, the church and the post office. Just after passing the bull ring, fork left at the sign for Ronda and Sevilla.

You reach a development of modern houses. When you reach a garish fountain turn left into Calle Libar. At the end of the street climb up onto a path that swings hard to the right and passes behind some

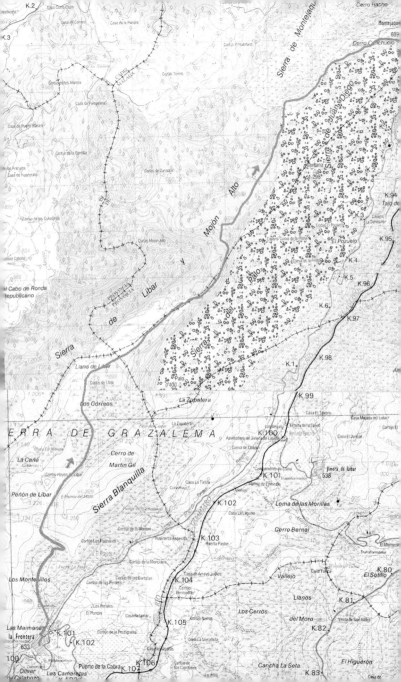

rather dreary blocks of flats. It then runs between two stone walls, bears left and descends to meet a dirt track. Go straight across the track and climb up a path that leads you past some ramshackle huts, through an old gate, and then climbs on up to a metal gate **(25 mins)**.

Just beyond the gate, you again meet the track. Turn right and follow it gently upwards. At the point where the track becomes concreted cut left onto a cobbled path (you'll see yellow and white P.R. waymarking) which soon reaches the track once again. Here bear left and at the next bend in the track (there is a rock with 'Líbar' painted in red) turn left onto a lovely old cobbled path that zigzags up the hill. There are fine views back to Cortes. Follow this path up until it meets again with a track **(1 hr)**.

Turn left onto the track, walk just 25 metres and then turn right onto another track that climbs

slightly. After just 25 metres it divides again and you should take the left fork that leads to a wire-and-post gate. Go through the gate. The path at this stage again becomes cobbled in parts. Down to your left is a flat area between the rocks where cattle may be grazing. The path climbs through an amazing sea of karst, skirting round the edge of the mountainside and soon you'll see a small farm-house over to your left. The path comes in to merge with a better defined track. Continue on your same course and - careful! - at the point where this track swings hard left to descend to the farm, you should head straight on, passing just to the right of a small depression. Here take the higher of two paths that you follow all the way up to the top of the pass where breaking over the top you'll see the flat-bottomed Líbar Valley down beneath you **(1 hr 30 mins)**.

You now descend all the way down to the valley floor. The path constantly divides but don't worry; as you head downhill, the paths again merge and you eventually reach a gate in a fence backed by a wall. Go through the gate and you'll pick up a path that leads out onto the flat, open floor of the valley which you will now follow north-eastwards to Montejaque. Head for a solitary old oak, pass it by to its right and continue following an indistinct path that shortly crosses a (dry) stream. A farm with solar panels comes into sight. Head for the farm and just past it, pick up a driveable track that leads along the right-hand side of the valley. When you reach a gate with a No Entry sign bear left along a stone wall and then swing right to resume your same course along the valley floor. Soon the track merges with the one you left at the No Entry sign.

Shortly a track cuts left to the Refugio del Líbar. You should continue straight ahead, go through a gate and carry on down the valley. The track becomes better surfaced and you pass through a stand of old oaks (this shady spot would be good for a picnic in the warmer months). The track runs on between the Sierra del Palo and Mojón Alto. After a short while, it descends slightly, passes a small ruin to left of the track, crosses a cattle grid, swings to the left and descends more steeply. You pass by a ramshackle pen and farm to the left of the track **(3 hrs 20 mins)**.

Just past here go through another gate before heading on up this broad valley floor towards another farm. Keeping to this track, you pass the farm and then a water tank and then a short section of uphill brings you to the top of the pass. Once you are over the pass, you drop steeply down a spectacular valley of karst. You cross a cattle grid and after a long descent come to a number of dog and chicken pens built against the right-hand side of the valley. Here the track swings sharp left, but you carry straight on down, with the

cliff still to your right. Soon you meet the first houses of the village. Follow this street all the way down into the village, bear round to the right just past the Las Yedras pub and you arrive in the main square of Montejaque (**4 hrs 45 mins**). Bar Alemán might be the right spot to slake your thirst.

Montejaque Circuit

Distance:	8 km (short) or 15 km (long).
Time Required:	4/4.5 hours (short) or 7/7.5 hours (long).
Rating:	Easy (short) or Med (long)
Map:	1:50000 Parque Natural Sierra de Grazalema or 1:50000 1050 Ubrique

The Walk of the Hidden Valley

This is one of the great walks of the Sierra, whether you choose the longer or shorter option. It takes you into the very heart of the Park, where flat bottomed valleys are surrounded by jagged outcrops of limestone and you are far away from roads and civilization. There are constant changes of scenery and passes that seem plucked straight from the pages of Carmen. If you walk this route, you will see why it was difficult for the authorities to bring the last of the bandaleros to heel. The long version has a long, steep haul up from Montejaque. It is beautiful but tough. You may prefer to wear long trousers because you encounter gorse and small holly oaks as you pick your way between the rocks. If you don't mind the odd scratch, you'll be fine in shorts. This route is rather more difficult to follow than some walks but it is well worth persevering. If you choose the long version of the walk you will have a fair amount of track to negotiate.

The Long Route.

The walk begins from the main square in Montejaque in front of Bar Alemán. Follow the left side of the church along under the palm trees and then bear right into Calle Nueva. Go left after just 20 yards into Calle Santa Cruz. You pass Bar Las Yedras. Follow this road all the way up through the village. You eventually leave the last of the houses behind and then pass by a number of kennels built up against the rock-face, to your left. Soon your road merges with a track that comes in from the right (**15 mins**).

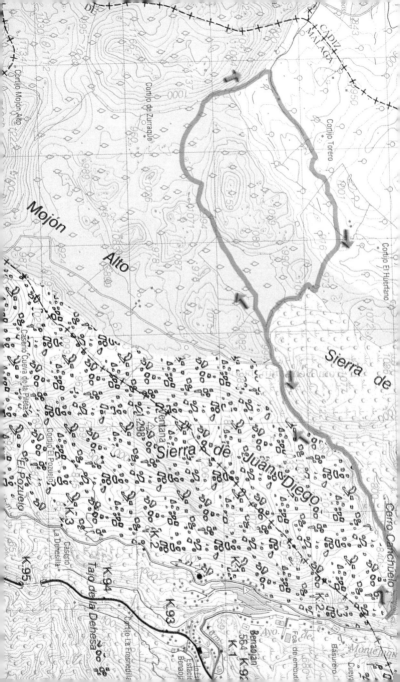

Continue straight up this track which climbs up the rocky-sided valley that runs between the Sierras of Juan Diego and Benaoján. You eventually cross a cattle grid then, at the very top of the pass, turn right off the track (opposite a small stand of oaks with a Coto sign in one of them). Climb up a track to a black metal gate marked Finca Jarastepa **(1 hr)**. See the continuation that follows.

The Short Route

Arriving in Montejaque by car from Benaoján, bear right by the '31 Pub' towards Sevilla/Algodonales.

After about 100 metres, turn left at a sign to Bar La Cabaña. Take the first road right immediately past Bar La Cabaña, where you will see a sign for Llanos del Líbar. The road climbs, bears sharply to the left towards the cliff face and then swings round sharply to the right, heading up the valley. You now climb for 3.5 km. A few hundred yards after cross-

ing a cattle grid, you come to the very top of the pass. Here you park in the shade of the old oaks, just to the left of the track, then climb up a track directly opposite you to a black metal gate marked Finca Jarastepa.

For a taxi to take you to this point ask for *"el punto más alto en el carril que va a los Llanos de Líbar, donde está la entrada a la Finca Jarastepa."*

Here the short walk starts and the long walk continues (timings are from the Finca Jarastepa gate).

Go through the black gate (or climb over the wall just to its right) and bear left between the oaks. Descending slightly, you come to a fenced off circular area (it surrounds a limestone 'sink' – a collapsed cave). Here the track divides and you fork left and shortly the track goes through a gap in a wall and emerges into a vast, flat open area surrounded by jagged outcrops of karst. Follow the track, now less distinct, all the way across this open area to the wall on its far side.

You pass a bull-dozed watering hole about three-quarters of the way across. Once you reach this wall bear right to a gate **(30 mins)**.

Here there is a shady spot beneath some oaks, a wonderful spot for a first rest. Go through the gate and bear left following a wall/fence along. The path climbs and then swings left, passes through a gap in a stone wall and emerges onto a small, flat, grassy area.

Careful! If you reach the fence at the end you have come too far. Here swing hard round to the right, looking for cairns. Enter a rocky, wooded area and begin to descend following an indistinct path, but there are cairns that help you find the way.

This is an exceptionally beautiful section of the walk. After descending for about 15 mins, you pass to the left of the ruins of a shepherd's hut and then go through an old wooden gate. Watch for the cairns, make sure not to climb at any point and you will

eventually emerge into another vast, flat, open area where there are a few clumps of oaks **(1 hr)**.

This area always reminds me of Africa, perhaps because the huge trunks of these oaks look rather baobab-like during the winter months when the leaves are down.

Careful! Looking west across to the the far side of the field, you'll see a wall that runs just above the level of the field, all the way across the hillside. Look for the point where this wall drops down, at its right hand end, to meet with the field and head for this spot. You should see a yellow and red oil drum as you approach.

There is a gap in the wall and from here you need to follow an indistinct, brownish path that climbs up and over the rocks marked by cairns. The path soon becomes clearer, a fence runs along to your left and, when you reach a large hollow where there is an animal pen up against the rock face, make sure to keep to the higher path, close to the fence **(1 hr 25 mins)**.

You are passing *El Hoyo de los Muertos* or Deadman's Gulch, where legend describes a bloody shootout between a group of *bandaleros* and the army. Skirt round and above it to the left. The path now leads up and over a low ridge. The countryside suddenly opens out once again and you'll see a farmhouse ahead of you (you will later be passing it by).

The path drops down and passes through a ramshackle gate, then passes by a fallen oak before it eventually comes to a low stone wall. Follow the stone wall along to the left and, where it ends, cross the (dry) stream

Just before you reach a well, swing sharp right and after a few yards you'll reach a track where you again bear right and head up the hill towards the farmhouse you could see earlier. The track crosses a cobbled *era* (threshing area), then passes between the farm and the animal pens beside it. Immediately past the second pen the track bears left, climbs, passes another wooden enclosure to its right, then descends to a wire-and-post gate.

Go through the gate; patience is required to untie this one. Careful! Go straight ahead for just 20 metres, then bear slightly left. You'll pick up an indistinct path marked by cairns that bears right and runs along the bottom edge of a small, open patch of ground before entering the forest. You'll see cairns again which lead you along an indistinct path that twists through the forest. At the far end of this enclosure, you arrive at another gate through a wall **(2 hrs)**.

This section - between this and the last gate – is the most difficult part of the walk to follow. (If you lose the way, remember that the gate really is there, just a few yards to the left of the wall's lowest point that coin-cides with the (dry) stream running the length of this enclosure.) Go through the gate. The path now climbs slightly and bears round to the right. Cairns occasionally mark the way. After just five minutes the, land-scape again opens out and the path runs just to the left of a low stone wall.

Continue to the far end of this field, keeping to its left hand edge then go through a rickety wooden gate then a second metal gate with a horse shoe closing device. You now bear slightly to the right and follow a (dry) stream across another open area and, after a few hun-dred metres, you will see a gap in the stone wall (for pigs) up ahead of you.

Just to its left is a second double set of gates. Go through here and continue on a similar course, at first heading for two oaks, out in the middle of the field. Pass these by and, bearing ever so slightly to the right, continue to the far side of the field where there is a large cairn by an old, twisted oak. Behind and just to the right of this oak go through a gap in a tumble-down wall and follow a path up through the rocks. It occasionally divides; you should stick to the main path.

Shortly you pass through a gap in a wall and emerge by a farm. Pass by the farm's garage/shed on your right, then pass between this and the farmhouse and on the other side you pick up a drivable track. It shortly reaches the sink that you passed at the beginning of the walk. Swing left and retrace your steps back to the gate where you began the walk **(3 hrs 15 mins)**. If doing the longer version swing, left onto the track and descend to Montejaque.

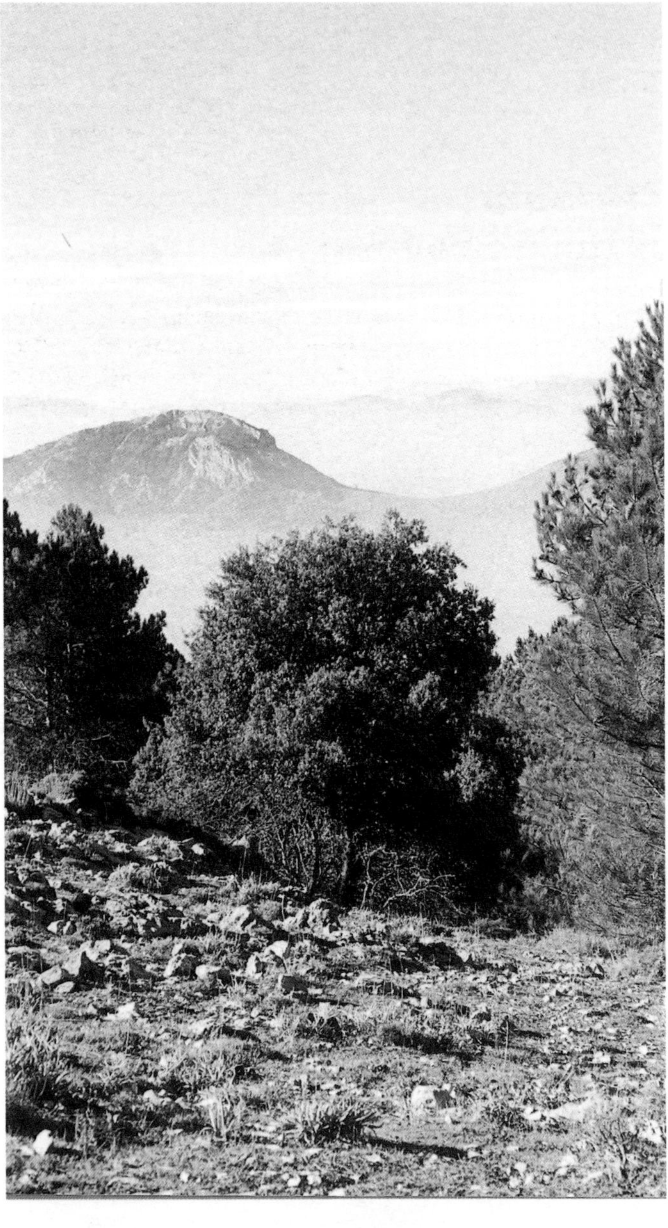

Montecorto Circuit

Distance:	13 km (14.5km with El Gastor)
Time Required:	6/6.5 hours
Rating:	Medium
Maps:	1:50000 Parque Natural Sierra de Grazalema or 1:50000 Ubrique (1050) & 1:50000 Olvera (1036)

The Walk of the Roman Mines

This unknown itinerary is a favourite of mine. There are dramatic changes of scenery and wonderful views of the Grazalema mountains and out across the Zahara Reservoir. It takes you through a completely unknown swathe of the Sierra, links two friendly villages and makes for a marvellous full-day excursion. The wildflowers are dazzling in springtime. You could halve the distance by ending your walk in the pretty village of El Gastor and taking a taxi back to Montecorto. Your route follows a mixture of farm tracks and goat paths, but it is easy to follow, except during the summer months when the thistles are up. There is a longish climb about half way through the walk, after you leave El Gastor, but your reward is a beautiful track that hugs the flank of the Malaver mountain. It winds through a wonderful old stand of oaks – the Romans mined for ore here – and leads you all the way back to Montecorto.

The Route

The walk begins from outside the town hall (*ayuntamiento*) at the entrance of Montecorto.

From here take the cobbled track signposted *campo de fútbol / bar La Piscina* that leads through the pine forest. At the end of the track, turn right into Calle Nacimiento and continue to the very end, dog-legging past no.54 that faces down the street. The paved road ends and becomes a red dirt track leading straight ahead (don't swing right onto a track that leads steeply up into the pine forest). There may be a chain across the

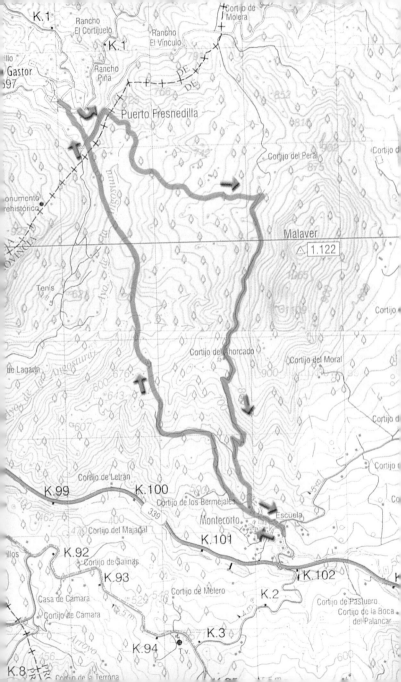

track after just a few metres. Continue along this track, ignoring another that swings left down towards a farm after just a few hundred metres. The track begins to climb and reaches a junction, where you turn left and continue on a fairly level track with a fence to your left. There are good views of Grazalema Sierra to the South. The track ends at a steep bank of red earth **(35 mins)**.

Follow a clearly defined path that climbs steeply up the bank. Continue on to a wire fence where you will see two tumbledown gate posts. Go through a wire-and-post gate and after 30m bear sharply right and climb up through the broom following a line of cairns.

The path becomes clearer as you climb upwards. Head for the lowest point of the ridge up above you. Again, look for the cairns. At the top you emerge on a flattish area where you have good views westwards across the valley. Here, by continuing towards the west you will

shortly see a solitary oak on top of a small rise.

The tree has a shepherd's shelter at its base. Head for the tree and just before you reach the base of the hill, swing right towards a ruined farm down in the valley following indistinct goat paths. As you descend try to locate the solitary oak mentioned in the next paragraph! The path becomes more obvious and you should see the occasional cairn. After crossing a (dry) stream, you reach the ruin **(1 hr 05 mins)**.

Pass just below, to the left of the ruin and, following cairns, cross another stream then bear right and climb towards the top of this second ridge. Again you'll pick up a line of cairns which leads you up to a solitary oak and, just behind it, to a wire-and-post gate through a fence. Go through the gate and turn left. Continue up, parallel to the fence.

The easiest path runs about 30 metres to its right. Pass through a rockier area

Pass through a rockier area before reaching the top of the ridge. Drop down on the other side and shortly you cross a (dry) stream. Here, begin to descend rather more steeply and cross a second (dry) stream.

At this stage, look for a line of poplars down in the river valley beneath you. Head on down and across a rather more open tract of land to the very last poplar on the right. Just behind it is a gate.

Go through the gate, cross the (dry) stream - *Arroyo de la Angostura* - and bear right on a dirt track. It climbs gradually at first, passes through a gate, and then becomes steeper. At one point it seems as if the track is about to end but you turn sharp left, then again sharp right and continue up along a better surfaced dirt track. It takes you up to the top of the ridge and to a crossroads **(2 hrs 15 mins)**.

Here you have a choice. If you intend to visit the village of El Gastor, head

straight across and drop down a steep road into the village. Remember you will need to return to this crossroads later. Bar Los Cuñaos or Los Cazadores is the best place for lunch.

If not visiting the village (bracketed timings assume that you have not) turn right onto a track that runs towards three transmitter masts. There are marvellous views out over the village down to your left.

After just 150 metres, take the very first track to your right and follow it steeply down to the bottom of the valley. You cross a small bridge, then go through a gate before coming to a farm **(2 hrs 25 mins)**.

Careful. Just a few yards before you reach this farm, turn right, pass between two rocks, and pick up a narrow goat path running parallel to the bed of the stream, now just to your right. You reach a fence where there is gate next to a white and black *coto* sign. Go through here, turn left and climb parallel to the fence all the way up until you reach a reddish track. You have about a half hour of climbing in front of you but if you keep parallel to the fence all the way up you can't go wrong. When you reach the track turn right **(3 hrs 10 mins)**.

The track will eventually lead you all the way back to Montecorto. You now pass through a fantastic stand of old oaks. Look out here for some depressions just to the left of the track. The Romans mined for ore here.

There are superb views of the Grazalema Sierra and the Zahara reservoir down to the right. Continue on, and you will eventually go through a green gate and, after about 100 metres, you will pass a spring just to the left of the track. You come to the farm of El Ahorcado **(3 hrs 40 mins)**.

Go through the gate leading into the farmyard (the large dogs may bark but they don't bite), turn left and follow the fence along to a second gate that leads you out of the farmyard. Follow this track back to Montecorto, eventually retracing the first part of the route that you followed this morning.

An alternative is to leave the track at the second point where it loops in to meet with the pine forest. You'll see a track leading into the trees and a cairn just to the left of the track.

You drop down to a clearing covered with small broken pine branches that the loggers left behind. Cross this clearing, continue descending and branch left at a first fork (to avoid a very steep track down) and, after just a few yards, turn sharp right.

Continue down the hill to another clearing. Here you cross a line of water troughs, then drop steeply down to a track in front of a green gated house. Turn left, pass the blue gates of El Tejar, and go down some steep steps to Calle Nacimiento. Retrace your footsteps to the Town Hall **(4 hrs 45 mins)**.

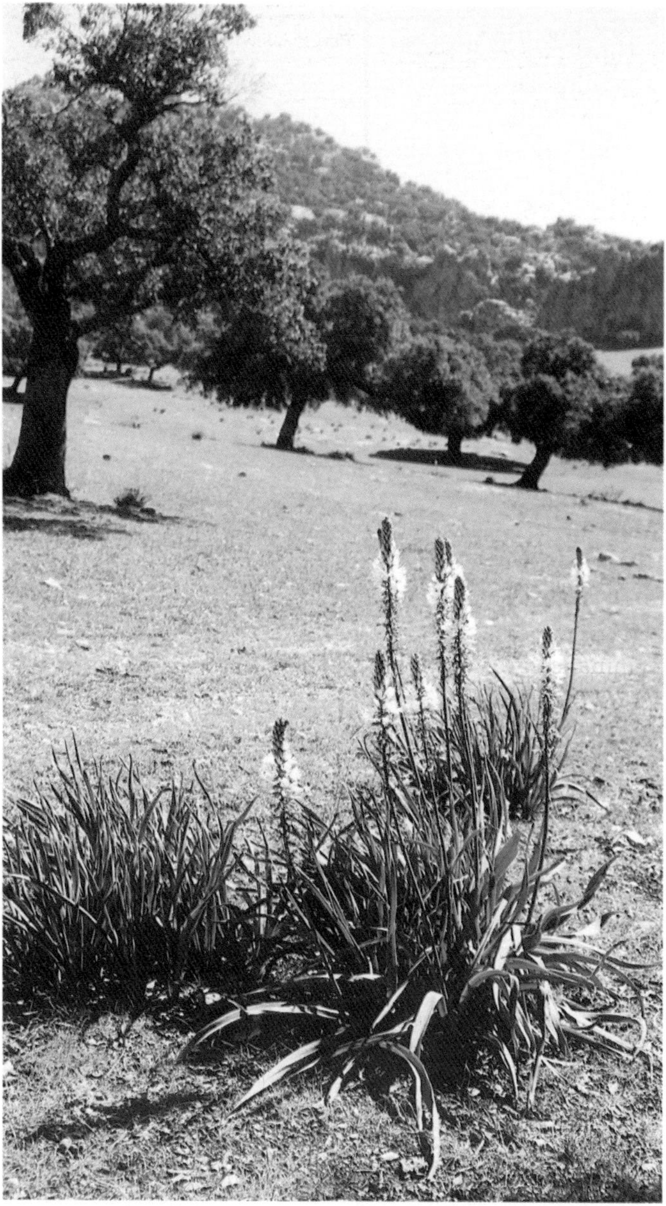

Distance:	14km
Time Required:	6/6.5 hours
Rating:	Medium/Difficult
Map:	1:50000 Parque Natural Sierra de Grazalema or 1:50000 1050 Ubrique & 1036 Olvera

The Walk of the Griffon Vultures

If you don't mind walking along tracks rather than paths, this is a truly great full day's walk. The hardest part of it comes first thing – a long pull up from 500m to 925m, following a well-surfaced track that hugs the course of the Breña del Agua stream. There are fantastic views of the Sierra del Pinar and the Sierra del Labradillo. The second half of the walk is nearly all down hill with views eastwards into the gorges of Garganta Seca and Garganta Verde, home to one of Europe's largest colonies of griffon vultures. You have a second steep climb for the last hour or so as you approach Zahara. The route links two of the Sierra's most attractive villages and each of them has somewhere good to stay. And the predominance of track rather than path means that you can forget where your feet are going and concentrate on the amazing views. But be sure to take plenty of water on this walk. You'll need to taxi to the beginning of the walk or back from the end of it, but this is easily arranged in Zahara or Benamahoma. See general section for details.

The Route

The walk begins at the bottom of the village of Benamahoma at the bus stop next to Venta El Bujío, opposite the furniture factory. From the bus stop, walk away from the village and take the first turning to the right. You will see signs for Molino de Benamahoma.. Cross the river and after just 40 metres or so, where the road swings right, you turn left, follow a fence for just 50 metres and then swing sharp right.

You now climb steeply up between two fences on a rough track (in parts made of building rubble). Go straight up (don't turn right in front of green gate) towards a white sign. Turn right and pass through a large rusting gate.

Don't take the lefthand fork just after the gate but stick to the main track and prepare yourself for nearly an hour and a half of climbing. You will be following the course of the Breña del Agua stream. You will soon pass through a metal gate (**45 mins**).

Continue climbing. About ten minutes later, the track swings sharply to the right and you pass by a ruined farmstead. Here the track swings left. Look for the occasional *pinsapo* amongst the oaks.

You will reach a goat pen and drinking troughs just to the left of the track. Careful! At the first large oak on the left, about 150m past the troughs, you will see a small cairn. Here turn left off the track (**1 hr 15 mins**).

Follow a path that climbs, at first indistinctly, but it soon improves. Cross a (dry) stream. The Breña del Agua is now on your left. The path runs more or less parallel to the stream and reaches an enchanting flat area, a good spot for a break.

Continue climbing to the top of the pass (**1 hr 30 mins**) where the path divides. Take the left fork and drop steeply down between the oaks. The countryside becomes much more open. You emerge into a rather flat area where there are fewer trees and a large table of limestone. Pass just to its left and the path reaches a second flatter and more open area.

Ahead of you is a gently convex hillside. Head for its left side: You will see a track cutting down across it. Your path descends to a second flattish area. Looking northwards, you can see a building with a white-posted gate. Head for this, keeping the Sierra Maragarita to your left.

You come to a gate that may be locked, but just to the left of it is a second wire-and-post gate. Go through here and carry on towards a small white farm. To your right, you'll see the Laguna del Perezoso, a watering hole that is sometimes dry.

Continuing along the same track you reach the farm where the track arcs round to the right. On a clear day this would be a great picnic spot. There are superb views northwards to the Sierra de Líjar and Algodonales.

Continue on this same track and look for Olvera in the far distance. Drop down on a well-surfaced forestry track through lovely stands of ilex oaks overgrown with hawthorn, wild olive, strawberry trees, ivy and gorse. Pass through a wire-and-post gate **(2 hrs 5 mins)**.

Continue your descent, always sticking to the main track. Zahara's Moorish castle comes into sight. The track continues down,

hugging the eastern flank of the Loma de los Albarranes. Eventually it swings sharply to the right, zigzags down to reach the valley floor. Here it swings left again and crosses a (dry) stream via a short, paved section of track. Go through another wire-and-post gate, then climb up through old groves of olives to El Puerto de la Breña **(2hrs 55 mins)**.

The track passes by a helicopter landing circle and you break out into the next valley. Ahead are the rocky crags of the Garganta Seca and, further to the left, the ochre cliffs of the Garganta Verde.

Once over the pass, the track bears left and descends, passing through another wire-and- post gate. Ignore a track leading to a farm to your left but rather carry on down the main track to a green gate **(3 hrs 25 mins)**.

Go through the gate and continue on down. There are spectacular views of Garganta Verde. The track

stream then, bears left and climbs upwards through the olive groves. Prepare yourself for today's second steep haul!

You reach a pretty farm to the left of the track with a palm tree and a citrus grove. Here, where the track swings left, just before you reach a green gate, turn right and follow a path that climbs steeply up through the olives. Cross a (dry) stream. The path improves here. Continue climbing and you meet with a steep concrete track that leads up towards a pylon.

You pass behind a row of modern terraced houses, then turn left and almost immediately sharp right and head up a street with a no-entry sign. The street bears left and you emerge onto a wider street that swings right then left. Follow this street and you will reach the main square of Zahara **(4hrs15 mins)**.

Distance:	11km or 14.5km (long)
Time Required:	4/4.5 hours or 5.5/6 hours (long)
Rating:	Medium or Med/Difficult (long)
Map:	1:50000 Parque Natural Sierra de Grazalema or 1:50000 Series L 1050 Ubrique

From Grazalema to Benaocáz

The Walk of the Goatherd's Leap

This is one of the Sierra's better-known walks and it fully deserves its reputation. There are constant changes of terrain and wonderful views to the west out across the campiña (glossary) of Jeréz and, on clear days, all the way to the Atlantic. Beautiful old stands of oaks, extraordinary karst formations, exceptional flora and good raptor-spotting possibilities make this a wonderful full day's excursion. You have a rather steep, unremitting climb if you leave from Grazalema centre (long version), so take a taxi up to the top of the pass if you prefer a more leisurely walk. From the Puerto del Boyar to Benaocáz, the walk is mostly down and along, with just a couple of short, uphill sections. Because of the popularity of this route, this walk is best done on a weekday. Get going by 9.30am to allow yourself plenty of time for stops and a picnic along the way and to make the 3.40pm bus from Benaocáz back to Grazalema (weekdays only). Or you could eat in the pretty village of Benaocáz. Bar La Palmera and Bar Las Vegas both have good food and great views, too.

The Long Route

The long version starts from Grazalema centre. Leave the village square by passing between the Unicaja bank and the *ayuntamiento* along Calle José María Jiménez. Bear left at the end of the street, pass Bar La Cabaña and climb to the top of the pretty Calle Real. Turn into Calle Portal, then take the next right and go up past a spring to the very

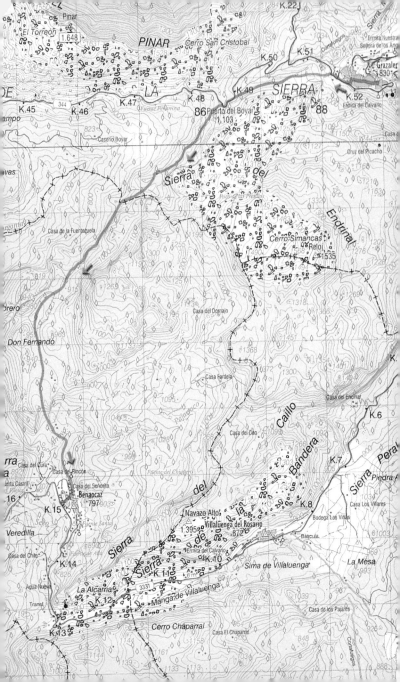

top of the village. Here you bear left, pass the Fromental cheese factory, then turn right onto the Grazalema - El Bosque/Zahara road.

Follow the right hand edge of the road. Soon you will pass by carparks to both sides of the road. From the one on the right there are wonderful views back across the terracotta rooftops of Grazalema.

Just before you reach a bridge across the river cross the road and head for a sign which says '*camino peatonal*'. Just behind it is a wooden footbride. After crossing the bridge you pick up a newly-laid foot-path which you now must follow all the way up to the top of the pass.

At first the path follows the right bank of the stream before crossing over and heading straight up on the valley. The road to the top of the pass is occasionally visible as it loops in close to the path. After a fairly unremitting climb up through an area of youngish

pine trees you eventually emerge into the car park at the very top of the pass.

Here go straight ahead toward a rusting 'peligro de incendio'sign (55 mins). Here pick up the itinerary below.

The Short Route

Take a taxi (or drive if leaving car at top of pass) to the very top of the pass at Puerto del Boyar between Grazalema and El Bosque. Here there is a large flat area to the left of the road and two signs 'Salto del Cabrero' and 'Peligro de Incendio'.

Just behind the first sign is a large gate with a second smaller wire-and-post gate to its left. Go through the gate and follow a dirt track gently down hill.

Ahead is a farm and beyond it the spectacular limestone cleft of the Salto del Cabrero (Goatherd's Leap). Make a mental note that you will later leave this formation to your right.

(Walkers sometimes swing too low, heading down towards the gap in the Salto, and have a hard climb back up to the correct track).

Just before the track reaches the farm, it swings sharply round to the right and here you cut off left, away from the track towards two old oak trees, beneath which are dog kennels; neither dog is to be feared. **(20mins)**.

Just past the second kennel, go through a wire-and-post gate and continue across a large flat area with magnificent old oaks. At the far end, you pass over a tumbledown wall and the path, occasionally dividing, winds through rather thicker under-growth. The secret is not to get too low. If in doubt, just keep left at any fork.

Soon you pass close to the cliff face to your left. The path then swings sharply right and drops down just to the right of a wall and a fence. After about 50 metres, go

through a graffiti-covered gate in the wall and follow the path downwards through thicker under-growth.

Careful! Don't drop too far to the right. If in doubt, keep left at any branch in the path, close to the base of the cliff. At times you see the Salto formation up ahead.

The vegetation becomes thicker and you occasion-ally have to stoop beneath branches. You come up to another gate with a walker symbol marking your way **(50 mins)**.

Go through the gate and bear right. Climb up and reach a flatter area, a nice spot for elevenses. The path now passes to the left of a fallen oak and climbs through an area where there are lots of brambles. Look for a fence running along to your right.

You reach a large open field with a water trough at the bottom. Go to the trough and bear sharp left and climb up following the same line as that of the trough.

Pick up an indistinct path that bears left and then right. It reaches the top of this more open area, then swings to the right and passes a fallen oak (don't take the path which bears left across a fallen wall).

The path winds round to the left to meet with a wall - and a gate. Go through here and follow the path roughly parallel to the wall. It leads you towards some lovely old oaks and then angles right, cutting across a more open stretch of land towards the back of the Salto, whose grey massif is now directly ahead of you. The path narrows and winds down through a very rocky tract of land.

Careful! This is ankle-twisting terrain. Watch for clumps of wild peonies between the rocks. Near the bottom of this rocky descent you climb over a wall then break out onto a vast, flat area by some oaks (**1 hr 40 mins**).

You are now at the eastern base of the Salto by

a small clump of oaks. Just beneath them, there is welcome shade, a good spot for a picnic. (You can scramble up to the top of the Salto from here. A lot of the climb is hands-on, there is no clear path and you should allow an hour to get up and down. First cut up to the right before swinging left. If you try climbing straight up it is very difficult).

From the picnic spot, turn to your left and walk directly away from the Salto across this vast open area. At the far end, pick up a path that crosses a wall and climbs gently up across another open tract of land where the vegetation is much sparser.

The path soon levels and Benaocáz comes into view. Look for a farm house up ahead. You need to leave it well to your left. Soon you begin to descend, passing just to the right of an old lime kiln (a sign explains how the lime was made). The path zigzags on down through the rocks to a gate **(2 hrs 15 mins)**.

With luck, you will spot griffon vultures perched on the cliffs above you to your right. Go through the gate and loop down to a flatter area where your path follows along beside a hawthorn-topped wall, passes through a green gate and then picks up a beautiful section of the old droverís path, which is cobbled in parts.

It crosses a stream by a pretty bridge, then swings right and climbs gently up towards the village. The path becomes a track. You pass an ugly housing development to your left. Continue on past Hostal San Antón. When you reach a garish villa on your left, branch left and continue to the village centre **(3 hrs)**.

To reach the bus stop, turn into the Calle San Blas by the Caja de San Fernando bank. Drop down, turn first left and descend again to the bus stop. The bus passes by at 3.40pm on weekdays, and 20 minutes later you alight in the main square of Grazalema.

El PARQUE NATURAL de LOS ALCORNOCALES & the GAUCÍN area

The area

El Parque Natural de los Alcornocales (the Park of the Cork Oak Forests) covers no less than 165,000 hectares of western Andalusia. It offers some of the best bird life in Europe, a whole string of beautiful white villages, wonderful places to stay and some of the best walking in Southern Spain. But, amazingly, we believe this is the first guide book in English to list walks in the area.

The Park – most of it lying within the province of Cádiz and with just a tenth or so falling within Málaga – points a finger down from Cortes de la Frontera towards the Atlantic. It is the most southerly of mainland Spain's protected areas, running all the way from El Bosque in the north to the Strait of Gibraltar in the south. The area encompassed within the boundaries of the Park corresponds roughly to that covered by the last reaches of the mighty Betica range, whose mountains gradually decrease in height as they stretch south towards Africa.

Like the province of Cádiz itself, the Park's character has been indelibly marked by its proximity to both the Atlantic and the Mediterranean. It receives astonishingly high rainfall considering its southerly position. This is primarily due to the prevailing westerly winds that are forced upwards as they meet the Aljibe, Blanquilla and Cabras Sierrras (glossary). But high levels of humidity are also maintained during the spring and summer thanks to the *Levante* wind. It gathers moisture as it blows hard across the Strait from North Africa and discharges it in the form of thick, morning mists that wrap themselves around the mountains and cloak the Mediterranean in a white mantle

before being burned off by the harsh, summer sun. These morning mists can provide you with a surprisingly cool start to some of these walks, even in summer when it would otherwise be too hot for comfortable walking.

This warm, humid climate has fostered abundant vegetation and the Park contains an exceptionally diverse flora, as well as some of Andalusia's most extensive stretches of forest. Most notable of all is the vast tract of cork oak forest which has given the Park its name. Nearly all the walks described in this chapter take you through stands of *alcornoques* (cork oaks). Stripped of their bark, their russet-coloured trunks have a beauty all of their own. These magnificent trees have long been a vital part of the local economy, not only for cork production but also as a source of food for the Iberian pigs. You are almost certain to come across them, grubbing for acorns, on any of these walks.

And these great swathes of wooded hill and mountainside are home to abundant wildlife. There are ginets, mongoose, martens, foxes, badgers and polecats, deer and much more besides. But what makes the area truly exceptional is the birdlife. This is one of the very best areas in the whole of Europe for ornithology, not only because of the great diversity of natural habitats but also because the seasonal migrations to and from Africa bring, literally, millions of birds straight over the Park. Be sure to pack your field guides and binoculars. You are bound to see eagles, vultures, buzzards, egrets, storks, kingfishers, owls and many, many more birds.

In order to make the walks as varied and as accessible as possible, I have added the area around Gaucín to that encompassed by this chapter. Although it is just outside the boundaries of the Park, it is a natural neighbour of the Alcornocales Park and of Jimena, too. It shares a similar climate, geology, and vegetation. And as this book goes to press, there are moves afoot to include it within the boundaries of the Park.

Gaucín or Jimena would serve as a good base for any of the walks listed in this chapter. Both are perfect examples of the classic Andalusian village, crowned by a castle and with a labyrinth of whitewashed houses spilling down the hillside. Gaucín has a large ex-pat community, a fact that is reflected in the price of both food and accommodation. In Jimena there are rather less foreigners. Benarrabá, on the other hand, is still virtually undiscovered and the recently built hotel (see accommodation) has fantastic views, friendly staff and friendly prices, too.

Other Walks

There are endless possibilities for further walks within the Park. The 1:75000 map could be a good starting point for deciding which areas to explore next. And you could link the walks described in this chapter with those of the Grazalema Park. A new GR route that runs all the way through the two Parks has recently been marked. Check for details at the Jimena tourist office.

The Hozgarganta river loop could be an easy first walk close to Jimena. Simply follow one bank of the Hozgarganta away from the village to a point just past Molino Felipe, then cross the river by a concrete bridge and return along the opposite bank. The walk would take about 1.5 hours and there are lovely river pools for swimming.

La Buitrera del Colmenar is a mighty, deep-sided gorge that is home to a large colony of vultures. You can reach it by walking north along the left bank of the Guadiaro from El Colmenar (Estación de Cortes), crossing the river and heading for La Casa del Conde, then dropping down towards the river. Never be tempted to enter the gorge during the wetter months.

The Laja Alta walk was one of the more popular walks in the Jimena area, taking you up to a jagged limestone outcrop and a cave with paleaolithic rock paintings. But access is currently under dispute. Check at Jimena hotels for details.

Accompanied walks: In Gaucín, Tiger and Melanie of Unseen Andalucia (Tel & Fax 952 15 33 30 or 650 41 51 34) organise (paying) guided walks. Patrick Elvin, a great walking enthusiast, organises regular walks. You can phone him for details (Tel 952 15 16 09). Patrick has many routes detailed on individual sheets that are on sale at the Gaucín town hall.

Maps

The only map currently available covering the whole of the Park as well as the Gaucín area is Parque Natural, Los Alcornocales (1998: Instituto Cartografía de Andalucía). But the 1:75000 scale is barely detailed enough for these walks. It could, however, be useful for planning your own walks.

The best maps are the standard 1:50000 map of the Servicio Geográfico del Ejército. The Gaucín and Benarrabá walks are covered by the 1:50000 series Cortes de la Frontera (1064). The two Jimena walks are both covered by the 1:25000 series Jimena de la Frontera (27-91). The La Sauceda walk ('the Queen's Bath') is covered by the 1:50000 series Algar (1063).

Best Places to Sleep

La Sauceda

Centro Recreativo Ambiental 'La Sauceda'.

Tel: 952 15 43 45

The former smuggler's hamlet of La Sauceda is as romantic a spot to overnight as you could hope to find. Accommodation is in simple thatched huts. Linen and towels are provided and there are barbecue areas for cooking. Approx. 30 euros for 2 includes wood for fire & transport of cases up to your hut. (Taxis: the nearest are in Jimena: Juan de Díos 956 64 01 91 or "Quini" 956 64 01 08). **Best Eats**: self-catering.

Jimena de la Frontera

Hostal El Anon.

Tel: 956 64 01 13

Fax: 956 64 11 10.

Five village houses make this interesting, multi-levelled hostal. Lively bar and restaurant serving Spanish and international food. Approx. 55 euros. (Taxis: Juan de Díos 956 64 01 91 or "Quini" 956 64 01 08). **Best eats**: here, Bar Cuenca or Restaurante La Parra.

La Posada Grande.

Tel: 956 64 05 78

Fax: 956 64 04 91.

Simple, comfortable place to stay at the far end of the village.

No meals apart from breakfast. Approx. 40 euros. (Taxis: Juan de Díos 956 64 01 91 or "Quini" 956 64 01 08). **Best eats**: two excellent, cheap-and-cheerful tapa bars right next door, or at Bar Cuenca or Restaurante La Parra.

Rancho Los Lobos.

Tel: 956 64 04 29

Fax: 956 64 11 80.

Simple accommodation and food at a converted farm just a mile or so outside Jimena. Horses and a huge pool. Approx. 50 euros. (Taxis: Juan de Díos 956 64 01 91 or "Quini" 956 64 01 08). **Best eats**: here, or as above.

Gaucín

Hotel Casablanca.

Tel & Fax: 952 15 10 19.

One of the very best places to stay in the area. Beautiful rooms, nearly all with views and a popular restaurant with a superb Belgian cook. Worth a splurge. Approx. 65–95 euros. (Taxis: José María 600 29 41 38 or Mundo 608 45 14 34). **Best eats**: here or at La Fructuosa.

La Almuña.

Tel: 952 15 12 20

Fax: 952 15 13 43.

The welcome is warm and genuine, the dinners *en famille* are always great fun and the views are simply heart stopping. 90 euros includes full English breakfast. **Best eats:** here.

La Fructuosa.

Tel: 952 15 10 72
Fax: 952 15 15 80.
Mobil: 617 69 26 84
Hard to choose between La Fructuosa and Casablanca as far as rooms and food goes. Beautiful decoration in the rooms. 80 euros inc. breakfast. (Taxis: José María 600 294 138 or Mundo . **Best eats**: here or at Casablanca. If the these are beyond your budget the bar next to the gasolinera has much cheaper rooms.

Benarrabá

Hotel Banu Rabbah.

Tel: 952 15 02 88
Fax: 952 15 02 08.
A modern hotel with amazing views from the front-facing rooms. Young, helpful staff and reasonable food at the restaurant next door. A good base for a longer stay in an untouristy village. 50–60 euros. (Taxis: Sebastian 952 150 164). **Best eats**: here.

Distance:	9 km
Time Required:	3.5/4 hours
Rating:	Medium
Map:1: 25000	Jimena de la Frontera (27- 91)

Jimena de la Frontera Circuit

The Walk of the Old Mill

This circuit makes for an easy half day walk out from Jimena. Although I have recommended allowing 3.5/4 hours for the walk, you could easily take far longer because the exceptionally pretty section of path leading down the Arroyo del Cañuelo should not to be rushed. There are rock pools for bathing and the old mill itself, about half way into the walk, is a heavenly spot for a picnic. On the higher sections of the walk, there are wonderful views back to Jimena and out across the beautiful Hozgarganta valley. And, apart from an initial steep section, there is not too much climbing involved. **Note:** This route is much more difficult in winter after heavy rainfall.

The Route

The walk begins in Jimena de la Frontera's Plaza de la Constitución, which is just to the left of the road as you arrive at the bottom of the village. Leave the square at the top left-hand corner near Disco-Bar Calem and head up Calle San Sebastian following signs for Hostal El Anon. Turn left into Calle Barrera, go along to the end and cross a small square into Calle La Vaca. Drop steeply down this street, then bear left into Chorro de la Calle.

Pass a spring and at the end of the road bear sharp left, then right, and drop down the hill past some ugly houses. Continue on past a sign marking the beginning of the Sendero del Río Hozgarganta. Your road merges with another, then crosses a bridge over the Hozgarganta river **(10 mins)**.

After a few hundred metres you reach a fork where you bear right up the hill. Don't swing left on the G.R.7! Pass between two wooden posts with faint red and white markings and the road levels. There are lovely views back to Jimena. Careful! 30m past an entrance to a farm to the left of the road, at a point where there are eucalyptus trees, you should turn right off the road at a faint red dot on a low wall **(25 mins)**.

The path climbs, passes between a stand of eucalyptus and arrives at a ruined farmhouse. Swing left in front of the farm and, just past a stone-walled pen, bear sharp right and pick up a rough track that loops steeply up above the farm. There are occasional red dots.

Soon the track ends. Swing right at a red dot and follow a narrow path steeply on up. Soon it crosses a track and leads up to the top of a rather more open, eroded swathe of hillside. At the top it

bears right and you again pick up a track that leads on and up through the oaks. This track soon peters out. Swing left and climb on up through the cork oaks to the top of the ridge, ignoring a large red square painted on a rock.

At the top of the ridge, there are great views up the Hozgarganta valley. Pick up a track that runs to the left, along the top of the ridge. It soon runs parallel to a wall and a fence, over to your right. The vegetation becomes sparser – again there are amazing views of the Park - and the track bears slightly left, away from the wall, then drops down to a fence with a wire-and-post gate **(45 mins)**.

On the other side of the gate, you'll see the tarmac road immediately ahead of you. Continue parallel to the road, just to its right, and you reach an indistinct track cutting directly in from the road. Bear sharp right onto this track (you should see a red arrow painted on a rock), drop over the top of the ridge and then bear left. There may be a chain across the track at this point. Follow this track all the way down through the cork oaks to the bottom of the valley. The track loops lazily downhill and you can occasionally cut off a corner. There are good views of the *lajas* (jagged ridges) on the other side of the valley.

The path becomes stonier and looser underfoot. Towards the bottom of the valley, wild olives begin to take the place of the cork oaks. Cross a (dry) stream and just before reaching the valley floor, the track loops hard to the left **(1 hr 25 mins)**. Here look right for a cairn where you swing right away from the track and then drop down through the wild olives.

The oleander-filled stream bed is to your left. (If you reach a concrete bridge across the Cañuelo, you have come slightly too far and should retrace your footsteps to the sharp bend described earlier).

The path is overgrown in parts but is easy enough to follow. Soon it crosses the stream, then follows on down the left bank of the Cañuelo. Cross the stream once again, this time via stepping stones. The sandy path improves as it winds through the rocks. There are rock pools.

You cross a third time at a place where the stream has been shored up and pick up a beautiful cobbled footpath. It climbs away from the river before swinging right, following a water channel. Soon you arrive at a derelict mill, a wonderful picnic spot, and just beneath you there is a great place to swim.

Just 75 metres past the mill, the path descends and crosses the river (bed). Look for a cairn. The castle of Jimena is visible up ahead. You pass another good bathing spot and the path climbs slightly away from the river into the cork oaks and passes between two huge rocks. At the next fork bear left, drop down and pass just to the right of a cork oak. The

Hozgarganta river soon comes into sight. The path again becomes cobbled and leads you through a wire-and-post gate (**2 hrs**).

On the other side of the gate, the path swings right and shortly follows a fence on a course roughly parallel to the River Hozgarganta, now on your left. Where the fence cuts uphill, your path bears left and eventually brings you back to the tarmac road. Turn left onto the road, cross the river and you have a final steep climb, back up into Jimena, to the Plaza de la Constitución (**2 hr 40 mins**), retracing the route that you followed earlier in the walk.

Distance:	10km
Time Required:	3.5 hours
Rating:	Easy/Medium
Map:1: 25000	Jimena de la Frontera (27- 91)

Jimena
Northern Circuit

The Walk of the Wolf and the Pigs

Constant changes of scenery and beautiful stands of cork oaks make this a good walk at any time of the year. On a clear day, you will be rewarded with views south to Gibraltar and - with luck - all the way across the Strait to the Moroccan Riff. You may well meet cork cutters if you do this circuit during the winter months. But the only wolf you are likely to meet is Wolf Zeiss, an amiable Austrian, who lives on a farm just outside of Jimena and who sometimes rides this way.

The Route

The walk begins at the bottom of the village of Jimena at the phone box opposite the Paseo de la Constitución, next to the Tienda Ortiz. Climb up this street and follow it all the way through the village. Leaving the houses behind, the road descends, passes a campsite on the left and reaches the road from Jimena to Algar (CA-3331).

Go straight across the road and climb up a wide newly cobbled pathway. The cobbling comes to an end and you pass through a wire-and-post gate. Continue up between two fields on a more indistinct path. It soon levels and then descends for a short distance. Views open out to your east of La Crestelina and of Casares hugging its southern end. Shortly you reach a wire-and-post gate. Go through the gate and turn right onto a track and you immediately come to a large metal gate (**40 mins**).

Go through the gate (it is sometimes tied closed), ignoring G.R.7 marker posts which lead uphill.

The track leads on upwards and the views open out to the north and to the east. You will now see *lajas* (jagged ridges) running down the mountainsides over to the right. You reach a point where the track divides and here you branch to the right (**1 hr**).

The track continues level for a short distance and then begins to gradually descend. Soon you have good views back to Jimena. Pass by a corral made of corrugated metal and brick. You may well see pigs grubbing beneath the oaks. Pass through a wire-and-post gate (possibly open) and continue descending. You now have views over the Guadiaro river valley to the village of San Pablo de Buceite. The track winds down and reaches a gate with a style on the left (**1 hr 35 mins**). Climb over and turn right onto a track that leads you back towards Jimena. Pass through a green gate, and continuing along the track you will cross a cattle grid. The countryside opens out and Jimena is again clearly

visible up ahead. Just past a 'Parque Natural' sign a road branches off right. You should keep to the main track which leads on towards Jimena and a barn on a hill surrounded by cypress and eucalyptus trees. Stick to the main track that eventually reaches the road again (**2 hrs 10 mins**).

Cross and continue on a tarmac road up to Jimena. It is a fairly tough slog uphill. Pass a house called La Bougainvillea and then, at house no. 7, swing sharp left, climb a pretty street and you emerge into a square in front of the church of La Misericordia. Continue to the top left-hand corner of the square and on up to the next street. Here, opposite Bar Pérez, take the street that climbs past Confecciones El Cachorro. Turn sharp to the left where the street divides, then at the end bear right, climb again and you emerge by a yellow post box. Turn left and follow the street back to your point of departure (**2 hrs 30 mins**).

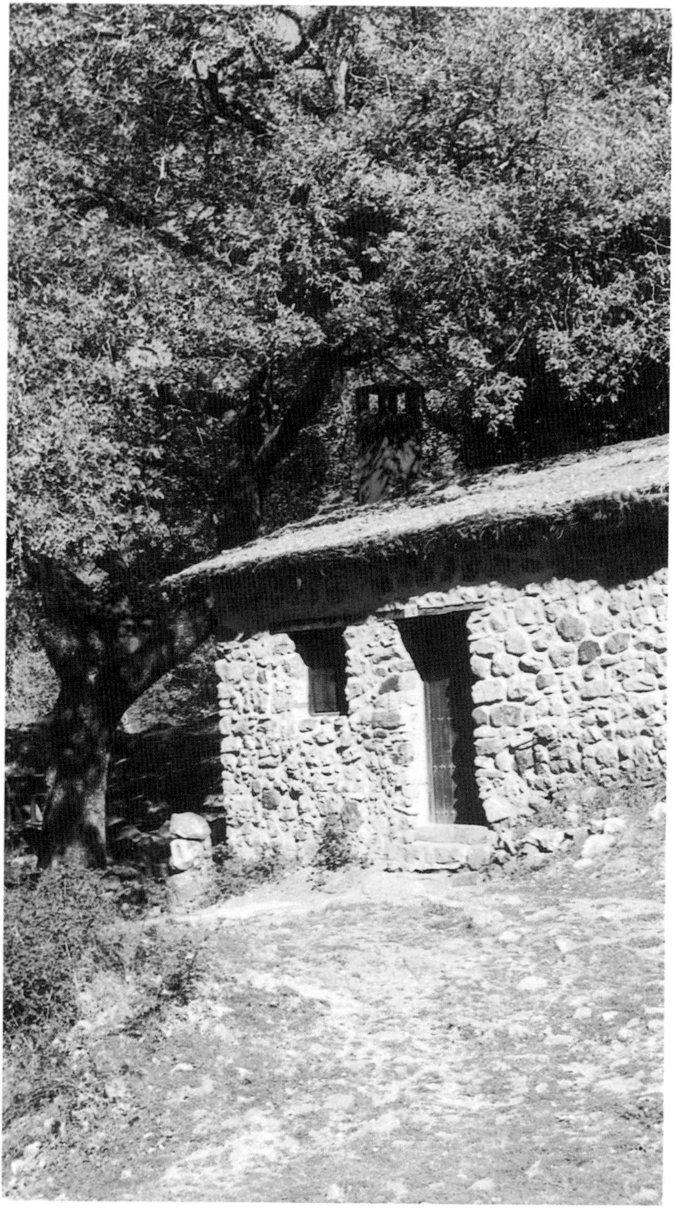

Distance:	11.5 km
Time Required:	4.4/5 hours
Rating:	Medium
Map:	1: 50000 Algar (1063)

The Walk
of the Queen's Bath

This walk takes you up to the rocky outcrop of El Aljibe (1092 m), the very highest point of the Alcornocales Park. You have a steep climb of nearly 500m up from La Sauceda but you are amply rewarded for your efforts. From El Aljibe on a clear day, you can see Gibraltar, Morocco, the mountains of Ronda, Grazalema and Gaucín, as well as any number of white towns and villages. Legend tells that during the final phase of the Reconquest, Queen Isabel bathed in the Pilita de la Reina, a recess hewn from a rocky outcrop just a few yards from El Aljibe. The walk is best done on a weekday, out of holiday season, and it would be fun to combine it with an overnight stay in one of the converted *chozas* (thatched hut) in the hamlet of La Sauceda (see accommodation section). This hidden settlement was one of the last redoubts of the smugglers who brought contraband from Gibraltar to the villages of Cádiz and Málaga provinces. Come on a weekday, out of season, best of all at new moon, and abandon yourself to the silence and the extraordinary night skys.

Getting to the start of the walk. Take the CA–3331 from Jimena de la Frontera towards Algar and Puerto de Galís. After approximately 22km, you'll see signs for *Nucleo Recreativo Ambiental La Sauceda* just to the left of the road. There is plenty of parking space on the opposite side of the road.

The Route

Cross the road and pass beneath the arched entrance of the *Nucleo Recreativo Ambiental La Sauceda*. Climb up past a sundial, cross a small bridge and you come to the reception area. You could book a cabin for the night

(your bags can be taken up to La Sauceda by landrover) and buy provisions from the small shop.

Continuing past the reception area, you reach a gate and a sign *Cabañas 1200m*. Follow a pretty path marked with white posts through the oak trees. It runs uphill, close to the left bank of the Garganta de Pasada Llana (marked on the 1:50000 military map Garganta de Rosada Llana and on some maps as Pasadellana!).

Soon you reach the hamlet of La Sauceda. Climb past the converted *chozas*, cross the stream by a small bridge and continue past more restored houses to the hamlet's ruined chapel. To its left you'll see an old bread oven.

Head for a solar panel to the left of the oven, climb for about 10 metres, then swing left onto a broad track that runs along through the cork oaks, hugging the right bank of the Garganta de Pasada Llana.

The track can be slightly difficult to follow because of its constant divisions. The secret for this first part of the walk is to keep the river close to your left. You pass by enormous moss and lichen-covered boulders, waterfalls, and huge cork oaks. The exuberant vegetation is a result of the unusual microclimate of the Park's steep-sided river valleys or *canutos* (see glossary).

After 500 metres, the track narrows and becomes a path that is occasionally marked by cairns. Cross a (dry) stream bed **(35 mins)**, pass beneath an enormous oak, then bear round to the right. You now cross a number of (dry) stream beds. If you look for the most clearly defined path and don´t drop too far to the left and keep watching out for cairns, you can't go far wrong. The path broadens and meets a track **(45mins)**.

Turn right onto this forestry track. The views suddenly open out across the heart of the

Alcornocales Park. Pass a water tank, just to the right of the track. The track continues to contour round the northern flank of the Sierra de Aljibe.

After about 10mins, you come to a wooden marker post, to the left of the track. Here you must branch left, away from the track, and pick up a path that climbs steeply up through the oaks.

Soon you pass between two huge rocks. An oleander-filled stream, El Canuto de los Sauces, is to your left. Cairns and marker posts help guide you upwards. Your path runs up to meet a clearer defined path where you bear left (there is a marker post) and continue climbing. Soon your path crosses El Canuto de los Sauces, bears right, and continues to climb.

After a very steep pull, you bear left. The path levels and the vegetation suddenly becomes much sparser. You come to two marker posts where you turn right onto a broad

track that continues to climb. Soon it arcs round to the left and heads across an open tract of land towards El Aljibe.

The path meets with a wall and a fence marking the provincial border between Cádiz and Málaga.

Follow the wall until you arrive at a rocky outcrop, La Pileta de la Reina. Beside it, you'll see The Queen's Bath, probably never a bath for a Queen but almost certainly a pre-historic burial niche. Pass through a gap in the wall and continue on up to the second outcrop, the 1092m El Ajibe (**1hr 45 mins**).

On a clear day, the views from here are sensational. The panorama takes in the Sierra de Grazalema, the Sierra de la Nieves, El Hacho above Gaucín, Gibraltar, the Strait and even the mountains of North Africa. This would be an obvious place for a long, lazy picnic.

When you come to leave, you have a choice. You

could simply retrace your steps. If you prefer to take a different route down, return to the gap in the wall by the Pileta de la Reina. Here, instead of crossing the wall, pick up a path that runs to its right, angling away from it at about 45 degrees. Cross an open area then descend towards another wall. Cairns mark the way.

When you reach the wall, follow it down, just to its right. You come to a sign for *Coto Privado de Caza* and just beyond it is a gate through the wall.

Go through here, continue straight on for just 10 metres, then bear right onto a path which continues to descend (to your left you can now see the path you followed earlier in the walk).

The path drops steeply down through the oaks. At a dead oak, bear left and carry on down, watching for cairns.

At first you follow a (dry) stream, crossing from one

bank to the other. Bear left away from it, cross a second (dry) stream and come to a much flatter area. Here bear right at a cairn and descend once again. Keep to the most obvious path.

Cross another (dry) stream by a large cairn and drop down to meet with the forestry track which you followed earlier in the day **(2hrs 30 mins)**.

Turn right onto the track, pass by the water tank once again and be ready to branch left off the track and retrace your footsteps back to your point of departure **(3 hrs 15 mins)**.

Distance:	7.5km
Time Required:	3 / 3.5 hours
Rating:	Easy/Medium
Map: 1:50000	Cortes de la Frontera (1064)

The Walk of Melanie and the Tiger

This easy half-day walk skirts round the mountain beneath the beautiful village of Gaucín and then cuts down to the ermita (hermitage) of Juan de Dios. There are some lovely sections of old path, a fair amount of track and even a section of Roman road, but you should prepare yourself for a fairly stiff final pull back up to the village. The walk is remarkable for the variety of vegetation and scenery that you encounter. There are wonderful views out across the Genal valley and Gaucín is always worth a detour. Melanie and Tiger, the friends who showed me this walk, know many other good routes in the area. See the "Other Walks" section for details.

The Route

The walk begins at the petrol station (la gasolinera) on the outskirts of Gaucín.

It is on the main road leading through the village from Ronda to Algeciras. There is plenty of parking space immediately opposite. From here head into the village centre, first passing bar La Bodeguita Chaparro then cafetería La Cruz. At the zebra crossing swing left along a narrow street. Pass the Molino del Carmen, and continue on through the village, passing between the Unicaja bank and the Mercado de Abastos.

Turn left at a sign for *consultorio*. You are now in calle Queipo de Llano. At the end of the street, just past house no 76, turn right, climb slightly, and then after just 20 yards swing left onto a track that immediately begins to

descend. The track drops down through groves of almonds, olives and carobs, skirting round beneath the village. At a fork **(25 mins)** by a large agave cactus, bear right, swinging away from the fence.

The track continues to descend and passes beneath a large white, rectangular building. When you reach a grove of carob and olive trees, don't swing left to a gate but continue straight on and you'll come to a more open area of meadow. A fence now runs to either side of the track.

Soon you pass a ruined farm to your left and just past it the track narrows and becomes a path. This beautiful section of path drops down and meets with another track **(50 mins)**, where you should bear right, up towards a cypress tree.

Here the track divides. Turn right here. Head uphill following pylons for 250m and at the next junction, where there is a carob tree to your left and pine trees ahead, turn left. You reach a large red gate.

Squeeze by just to the right of this gate. Views open out across the Genal valley to the mountain of La Crestelina. Continue on down this track and pass a rocky area where bee-eaters nest. Still descending, pass twice beneath the electricity lines and you then come to a fork. Here bear sharply right (it is marked by a cairn on the right) up towards the mountain of El Hacho. You are following a recently bulldozed track. Soon you meet with a better-surfaced track where you should continue on your same course, climbing slightly, between oak and pine trees.

You now head on up towards a pylon. Soon the path becomes rockier. Follow the main track to the top of the hill and when you reach a green pylon swing left and drop steeply downhill. Look for the barrel-vaulted ermita beneath you. Again there are lovely views of the

Genal valley. You arrive at an open area with the Chapel of Juan de Dios to the left **(1 hour 20 mins)**.

The chapel is the destination of a summer romería (glossary), when the villagers bring the Santo Niño (the Christ Child) down from Gaucín. This would be a good place to break for a picnic.

When you come to leave, head directly away from the main entrance of the chapel and you'll pick up a wonderful old section of track that passes just to the right of a huge carob tree before climbing up between two almond groves.

Pass by an unusual group of modern buildings with extraordinary wafer-bricked columns to the left of the track. Continue on and upwards along this narrow path which soon comes up to meet with a broader track. Here go straight on and continue climbing. Soon you'll see the Gaucín-Casares road down beneath you.

Shortly another track cuts across the one that you are following, down towards the tarmac road. Ignore this track but rather continue straight ahead. The track climbs steeply away from the road, bears round to the right and leads up and over a ridge where Gaucín comes into sight. Continue straight on up towards Gaucín, following a line of pylons.

Prepare yourself for a steep climb! Soon you pass by Finca El Alborrán to your right and a little further on a track cutting in to El Nobo, also to your right. Continue straight on upwards to the first houses of the village where the track becomes paved. You pass by the restaurant 'La Fructuosa' and come to a junction. Here you turn hard left along a one way street and go back through the village to your point of departure **(2 hours 25 mins)**.

Distance:	11km
Time Required:	4.5 hours
Rating:	Medium
Map 1: 50000 :	Cortes de la Frontera (1064).

The Walk
of the Cork Cutters

This route makes for an easy half-day walk out from Gaucín. It is easy to follow, the views seem to change with every turn in the path and the variety of birdlife is extraordinary, especially during the spring and autumn migrations. There is a steepish haul first thing as you head up the north-eastern flank of el Hacho, and another at the end of the walk when you head back up to Gaucín. There is a longish section of forestry track mid-walk where you can abandon yourself to the wonderful views out towards the Sierra del Pino and the Sierra del Líbar. Your feet can take care of themselves at this point! You may meet with teams of men cutting back the cork oaks on this walk. The trees are particularly memorable when seen just after their nine-yearly cut.

The Route

The walk begins at the Campsa petrol station – *la gasolinera* – on the outskirts of Guacín. There is always parking space directly across the road.

By the entrance of the petrol station (at the Guacín end), head along a track that leads between a row of modern-built houses and two green garage doors. Directly opposite house no 16, just before you reach a gate to your left made from two railway sleepers, climb up a dirt bank and pick up a good path which runs just to the left of a line of eucalyptus trees.

Pass to the left of a white-posted paddock and begin to climb. Soon the path runs between two fences and climbs up between groves of olives

and almonds. Ignore a track that branches off to the right (**5 mins**): continue on up.

Ahead you will see the track you'll be following, cutting across the northern flank of El Hacho. Soon you'll see a second track leading, down to a farm. Again ignore it, keep left on the main track and continue to climb. Shortly the track swings hard to the right.

It becomes rather more overgrown as it passes just to the left of a large, statuesque rock. From here there are good views down to Gaucín. Careful! The track ends (a path zigzags away to the left). Drop down a steep section of loose path and pick up another path that runs just to the left of a fence and climbs gently up to a pylon at the top of the ridge.

Here go through a wire-and-post gate then continue on your same course, descending on a rather indistinct path that runs down through oaks and

conifers, just to the left of a fence. After a final steep descent, the fence drops down to meet with another fence, where there is a wire-and-post gate. Go through the gate, turn left and follow a track across an open tract of ground.

The track bears right downhill and – careful!- after some 200 metres, you'll see a drinking trough on the other side of the fence, to your left. Here go through a wire-and-post gate and, just past the water trough, bear left up the hill.

Just before you reach a fence, look for a small concrete well cover. Here, bearing right, pick up a narrow path that runs more or less parallel to the green-posted fence, now above you to your left. The path climbs gently through the oaks, and views open up across the valley to Cortes de la Fontera and the Sierra de Líbar.

Cross a (dry) stream and you shortly come to a rocky cutting/defile, to the left of the path. Bear left here, following the path through this breach in the hillside. On the other side, you'll again be just beneath the green–posted fence.

The path begins to descend and, after crossing a (dry) stream, loops round to the right. You now lose the fence.

Shortly you come to an indistinct fork. Keep left, wind steeply down, pass just to the left of an old oak, and then cross a (dry) stream.

You soon come to a green fence which cuts directly (and illegally I believe) acros the path. Here bear right down the hill just to the right of the fence.

After crossing the second of the two small (dry) streams cut down and away from the fence at 45 degrees.

After just 25 yards bear left on a more clearly defined path and you meet with a track leading up to a newly-built house. Here turn right

down hill towards a pylon/ transformer.

Just beneath the pylon (**1 hr**), two tracks bear right and another left. Ignore the lower track to the right sign posted for El Peso and turn sharply to your right and head along a broad forestry track that you will now be following for the next forty minutes or so.

The track gradually descends. There are wonderful views. Pass a quarry and then a goat farm, both just to the right of the track and then come to a junction. Carry straight on here. Don't turn left down towards Finca La Capellania.

The track contours lazily round the valley and Gaucín shortly comes into view up ahead of you.

Continue along the track (ignoring a track leading temptingly up to the right) and soon you cross a tributary of Garganta de las Palas, at a point where the track loops sharply left.

Just a few hundred metres further on, cross the Garganta de las Palas itself. The track bears hard to the left once again, and crosses a third stream bed.

Careful! Watch out for a small white sign for Camino de Gaucín a Cortes in a tree just to the right of the track **(1hr 45 mins)**.

It is easily missed. It is opposite an oak tree whose split branch has dropped down to meet with the track's dirt bank. There is also a small cairn to the left of the track. Here bear sharp right away from the track and follow this track steeply up through the heather, gorse and lavender.

It winds up through the cork oaks and eventually passes through a wire-and-post gate where the path broadens and soon comes up to meet with a better-defined track. Here you bear right, following a fence and soon you pass by the Shambala Buddhist centre, just to the left of the track.

After passing an ugly discotheque, you come up to meet the Ronda-Gaucín road. Cross over here, go right past the bandstand then take the first road to the left that leads up to the village. It is signposted *centro urbano*. Go all the way along Calle Queipo de Llano.

At the end of the street bear right, pass the kiosco (kiosk), and go straight across at the next junction, passing to the right of Modas Teresa. Go all the way along this street and at the very end bear right, pass the Guardia Civil headquarters and meet the Ronda-Gaucín road. Just opposite you is the garage where the walk began **(2 hrs 30 mins)**.

Benarrabá Circuit

Distance:	11 km
Time Required:	5.5/6 hours
Rating:	Medium
Map 1: 50000 :	Cortes de la Frontera (1064).

The Walk of the Vizir's Garden

This lovely figure-of-eight makes for a longish day's walk and links two beautiful, little-known villages. The majority of the walk takes you along forgotten donkey paths and there are wonderful views out across the Genal valley and south towards the Mediterranean. If you do the whole route, you have three fairly stiff climbs, but the path is easy to follow and there are shady sections beneath the oak and the chestnut trees. You could shorten the walk considerably by simply swinging right before you cross over the Genal. But this would mean missing Genalguacil, an exceptionally pretty village that is a highlight of the walk. Be sure to visit its beautiful square and restaurante El Refugio, the perfect place to break for a mid-morning coffee - or lunch if you are setting out later.

The Route

The walk begins at hotel Banu Rabbah at the far side of the village of Benarrabá. From the hotel, walk back towards the village, passing the football pitch and then the school. Just past the school, opposite a line of tiled benches, turn right down Avenida Miguel Pérez Delgado and then right again into Calle Sol.

The street bears sharply right. Pass a fountain and, just to the right of house no.16, branch off onto a narrow path that drops down the hill, away from the village. You'll see a sign for Ruta Río Genal. At intervals you'll see white arrows marking your way.

The path widens and you continue your descent. You come to a large oak in the middle of the path. Pass by

it to the right and continue along the deeply worn path. It soon merges with a track **(30 mins)**.

Here you bear right, go through a gate (sometimes open) and after just 20m – careful! - turn left off the track (a rock marks the spot). The path becomes looser underfoot and more overgrown. It loops steeply down to meet with Arroyo del Infiernillo. Cross it and bear right along a track.

Soon you cross back to the right bank, descend, then cross back once again to the left bank and now continue gently on down, leaving a fenced-off paddock to your left. Cross the Arroyo one final time and the track runs up to a bridge across the Genal.

Cross the river (there is a nice spot for swimming here) and then swing immediately left along a track that hugs the right bank of the Genal. Don't climb over a stile that leads to Finca La Escribana (marked on some maps as Casa Los Limones).

Drop down a short section of (dry) stream bed and continue along the Genal's right bank. There is a thick hedgerow on your right. Very shortly you reach a sandy area where you swing right through the undergrowth, away from the river, and again pick up the old footpath from Benarrabá to Genalguacil **(55 mins)**.

Climb steeply once again and, after about ten minutes, cross directly over a track and continue on up through the oaks. Soon you cross the track once again. After a more overgrown section of path, views open out across the Genal valley. You again meet the track by a white and red-gated post **(1 hr 25 mins)**.

Cross the track a third time and, just before you reach a gate, bear right and once again pick up the footpath. It descends slightly, levels and then arcs round the head of a gully before coming to an old farmhouse. Just past this farmhouse, turn left by an agave cactus. The

path winds steeply up-
wards away from the farm.
Pass a (dry) spring and
soon your path merges
with a track. Pass a tennis
court and then arrive at a
junction at the outskirts of
the village. Turn right and
follow the tarmac road into
the village centre, passing
a tiled plaque

At a 30km speed limit
sign, keep right, pass a
spring and then go all the
way along Calle Real,
passing the Unicaja bank,
then the Casa Consistorial,
to the church **(2 hrs)** where
you should turn right.

You arrive at the village's
beautiful main square, La
Plaza de la Constitución.
On the far side you'll see
an arched doorway leading
to the beautifully located
restaurant El Refugio, a
perfect spot for refresh-
ments.

After a drink or meal,
retrace your steps back to
the Plaza and leave it by
the street running to the
left of the church, the same
one by which you entered
earlier. At the far end, just

to the left of a mirador
(viewing point), go down a
concrete track and –
careful! - after just a few
yards swing right at a sign
for Camino de Casares.

Pass Finca Bancaliyo and
drop steeply downhill,
always sticking to the main
path. You come to a farm
just to the right of the path
where there is a (dry)
watering hole immediately
in front of you. Keep left
here and carry on down
past another small, white
building.

The path widens and you
can now see the river and,
on the far bank, the ruined
arch of an old (Roman
according to the locals)
bridge. Your track drops
down to meet with another
track. Turn right here and
continue on down. The track
soon loops hard left and
leads you down to the river.

Head across the pebbly
river bed towards a farm
and, before you reach it,
cross the river Almarchal
(in the wetter months you
may need to remove your
boots). Once you're over the

river (**2 hrs 30 mins**), bear left and then, some 20m before you reach the ruined arch, swing up to the right onto a narrow footpath. It climbs steeply away from the river between prickly pears.

You reach a gate where you bear left and continue on up. Shortly you'll come to a track where you bear left. The track now contours round to the right, climbing more gradually before it levels.

You come to an abandoned farmhouse where the track divides. Fork right here, pass another ruin ignoring a well-defined track that leads off to the right. Your track loops down the hillside towards the river Almarchal. Just before it reaches the river you meet with another track. Turn left here and cross over the river bed (**3 hrs 10 mins**).

The track now runs indistinctly up to the bridge you crossed earlier in the walk. Cross back over the Genal and turn left onto a broad track. At first it hugs the river's right bank but soon it begins to angle away from it, climbing steeply. Cross a cattle grid and after just 50m pass by a spring.

You could replenish your water bottle here as you have a steep climb ahead. Carry on up the main track and, after about a quarter of an hour, watch for the point where a line of pylons runs up to meet with your track(**3 hrs 35mins**).

Ten metres past the second pylon, turn right off the track. There is a sign for Benarrabá. Pass between two drain covers, bear slightly left and climb. Shortly afterwards you come to another white arrow on a young cork oak. Go straight ahead here, ignoring a waymarked path to the right and, after 50m, pass through a wire-and-post gate. Follow the path steeply up to the village until it meets with the road by the college you passed earlier in the walk. Turn right here and return to the hotel (**4 hrs**).

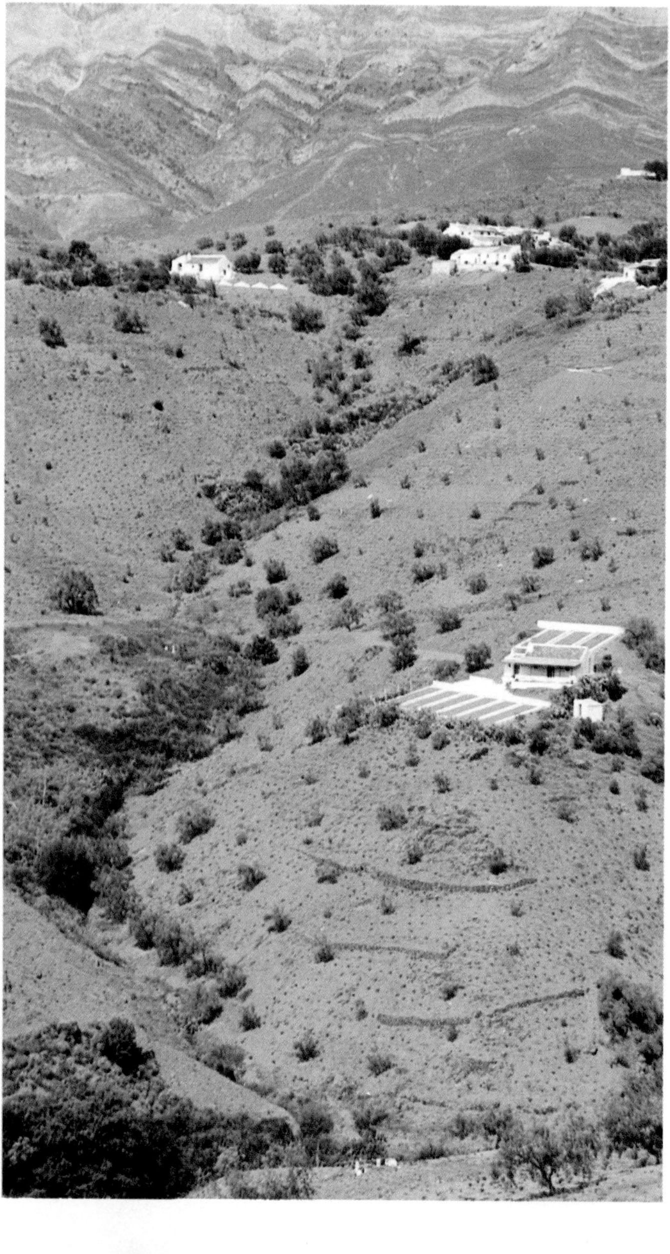

LA AXARQUÍA

The area.

The Axarquía was the name given by the Moors to the swathe of land just back from the Mediterranean which stretches for some 50km east from Málaga towards the Sierra Nevada. Axarquía literally means "the land to the East" – as opposed to the Algarve, "the land to the West".

The landscape is rugged, often spectacular. A series of valleys have cut deep courses through the chain of the Tejeda mountains in their rapid descent to the sea. There are marked differences in climate and vegetation between the higher passes and the coastal fringe and the region offers exceptionally varied walking. A belt of white villages, nearly all of them with views down to the Mediterranean, pepper the southern flank of the mountains. Rising up behind them to over 2000 metres, the Sierra de Tejeda provides a stunning backdrop, especially during the winter months when there is often snow on its higher reaches.

The tortuous nature of much of this area meant that it attracted its fair share of *bandaleros* who worked the passes that lead through the mountains from Granada. And as late as the early fifties, there were still bands of Republicans at large who had fought on after the Civil War. They, too, were able to make the mountains a formidable redoubt.

The most attractive part of La Axarquía is its eastern end and the walks in this chapter are all in the beautiful area of mountains and lush river valleys surrounding Cómpeta. The town is as *andaluz* as you could hope to find – with whitewashed walls, terracotta tiled roofs and narrow backstreets with balconies brimming with geraniums. There are a number of exceptionally friendly bars and restaurants concentrated in and around the pretty main square. Even though the town has been discovered by many other northern Europeans, it makes a good base for any of the walks described in this chapter.

The contrast between the land to the north and south of the village could not be greater. Beyond the very first ridge above Cómpeta, the landscape changes dramatically. Before you is a vast arena of limestone peaks where there is virtually no sign of human habitation. This is in marked contrast to the land between the village and the sea that is extensively cultivated and sprinkled with numerous small farmsteads.

Cultivation is aided by an exceptionally benign climate and careful irrigation. Many of the water channels date back to the Moorish period. The hillsides, especially round Cómpeta and Canillas, are covered with olive groves and vineyards where the sweet Moscatel grape is grown. Nearly all the farms here have one or more of the characteristic platforms (*secaderos*) that are used to sun-dry and fortify the grapes used to make the famous *vino de moscatel*. A tasting should be an obligatory part of any visit but, unless you are a lover of really sweet wines, be sure to ask for *seco* in the bars and restaurants.

Many of the walks described here take in sections of the lush, sub-tropical river valleys so characteristic of the lower Axarquía. Everything, it would seem, will grow here. There are groves of citrus, avocado, mangos, pomegranate, and even custard fruit, lichees and sugar cane. These fertile valleys provide a welcome respite if you are walking during the hotter months. The section of the river valley north of Canillas is particularly attractive.

In spite of a growing numbers of expatriates who have made the area their home (you'll spot a fair number of villas amongst the farms), the villages have still managed to retain their Spanishness. The exception is, perhaps, Frigiliana that has become a popular destination for coach-trips up from the coastal resorts. The village is best avoided during the middle part of the day, but it does regain much of its dignity by the evening and is, it must be said, a very pretty village.

The variety of scenery you will encounter on your walks here is remarkable and you will meet with few other walk-

ers on your rambles. The benign climate means that this is an area well suited to winter sorties. Málaga can be reached in little more than an hour.

Other Walks

Close to Cómpeta. The guide book *25 Walks in and around Cómpeta* lists a number of short walks in the area, although the maps can be confusing. Far easier to follow are the walks described by Elma Thompson in a series of leaflets called *Exploring La Axarquía* (you can find it in shops in Frigiliana). Most of her routes leave from Frigiliana. One of the best is the Limán trail that leads from the village to the Maro caves.

La Maroma. The highest peak of the Sierra Tejada, La Maroma reaches an impressive 2065 metres. The ascent of the mountain is not technically challenging but it does take a full day. The easiest route leaves from Canillas de Aceituno and follows the old Camino Arriero de la Nieve, the route once followed by muleteers who in pre-refrigerator days brought ice down from covered pits in the high sierra .

Maps.

The best maps of the area are the standard 1:50000 map of the Servicio Geográfico del Ejército, Series L. The walks described in this section are covered by sheet (hoja) Zafarraya 18-43 and sheet (hoja) Vélez-Málaga 18-44. The Marco Polo bookstore just off the Plaza de Almijara in the centre of Cómpeta (952 51 64 23) generally has both of these maps in stock.

Best Places to Sleep

Cómpeta

Casa La Piedra.
Tel: 952 516 329 or 657 056 166.
Two bedrooms in an interesting old house in a pretty square looking down to the sea. Sandra, the British owner, knows many of the walks in the area and has created a truly beautiful home. Approx. 50 euros. (Taxis: Paco 952 51 60 56 or Cesario 952 51 62 05). **Best Eats:** El Pilón, Cortijo Paco.

Hotel Balcón de Cómpeta.
Tel: 952 553 535
Fax: 952 553 510.
A good second best if Casa de Las Piedras is full. Good rooms with views down towards the Mediterranean. Be sure to book a room with a terrace. Approx. 60 euros. (Taxis: see above). **Best Eats**: see above.

Alberdini
Tel: 952 516 241.
On top of a high ridge just outside of the village with exceptional views and some interesting 'organic' architecture. Best in warmer months: the heating is a bit hit–and-miss. Approx. 40 euros. (Taxis: see above). **Best eats**: here or see above.

Canillas de Albaida

Finca El Cerrillo.
Tel/Fax: 952 030 444
A converted olive mill just outside of the village. Great food and atmosphere, the nicest place to stay in the area. 90 euros. Taxi: José 608 952 880. **Best Eats:** here or restaurant plaza.

Sayalonga

Village Houses.
Tel: 952 535 206.
The tourist office has details of a number of village houses for rent, either for just one night or for a longer stay. Prices vary according to size of house.

Árchez

El Mesón Mudejar
Tel: 952 553 106.
Five simple rooms above a popular restaurant and by the church in the centre of the village. Great value at 40 euros. **Best Eats**: here. Try the lamb in honey sauce.

Cómpeta Circuit (via Árchez and Canillas)

The Walk of the Low Axarquía

This easy circuit offers you a good introduction to the hills and valleys around Cómpeta and passes through two of the region's prettiest villages. There is a lovely section of path along the river Cájula that you need to cross several times. In the wetter months, you may need to take off your boots and socks. A good plan might be to set off mid-morning, at about 11am, so that you arrive in Canillas in time for an early lunch in the square. From here it is a very pleasant ramble back to Cómpeta by way of the beautiful, irrigated terraces where several subtropical species of fruit trees flourish. You can easily see why La Axarquia was seen as a land of plenty by the Berbers who first irrigated these fertile valleys. The walk takes in a mixture of path and track with just a couple of short sections of tarmac when you pass through the villages of Árchez and Canillas

The Route

The walk begins in Competa in the Plaza de la Almijara, next to the church of Nuestra Señora de la Asunción.

Leave the plaza at its top, left-hand corner and go along the Calle de San Antonio. You pass the Museo del Jamón and the consultorio, the hotel Balcón de Cómpeta and then the Chapel of San Antón. Just after the chapel, you come to a three-way split in the road.

The street that you have been following bears right, another goes left, but you should take the middle

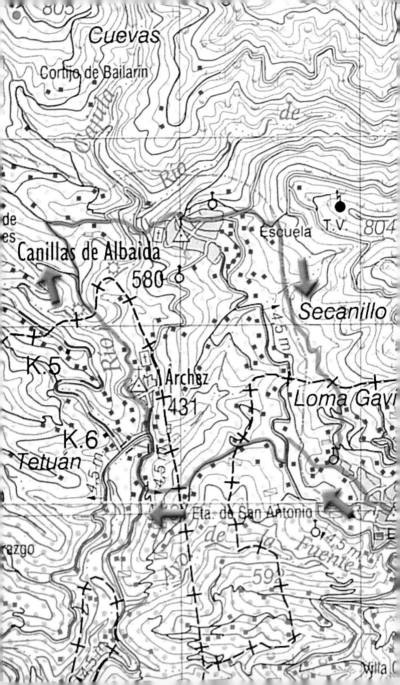

way, a concrete section of road that drops steeply down and after just 20 yards becomes a path. It leads you down through groves of citrus, crosses a stream and then comes to fork in the path. Take the left fork that leads you towards a modern house with a row of cypress trees to its right

The path passes just to the right of the house and then meets with the Competa/Canillas road. Turn left here and continue until you are opposite a house with a white bench, Casa Paraíso. Here turn right off the road by the Jaral vineyard (tastings possible) onto a track. The first section is paved. Continue past Casa Mimosa sticking to the main track. Ignore a track that leads off to the right.

Soon you begin to descend through the almond groves and come to a point where a fence with green netting runs just left of the track. Turn right here onto another track that drops steeply down through the

terraces of olives, almonds and vines. Soon Árchez comes into view. You pass beneath some pylons and then you will see a line of concrete posts to your left.

Leave the track at this point and pick up a narrow path that drops down, indistinctly at first, following the line of pylons. It soon improves and leads you down past stands of agave, cactii and prickly pears. You pass a house to your left. Here the path becomes paved for a short section. You come to a tarmac road **(45 mins)**.

Turn right here and soon you'll reach the outskirts of Árchez. Go past Bar Avenida, the *consultorio* and *ayuntamiento* and you arrive at the Plazuela Mudéjar with its beautiful 13th century *almiñar* (minaret). Leave the square via the narrow street just to the right of the *almiñar*. It passes a ceramic painting depicting the village's history.

Turn right at the end of this street onto a road that

hugs the right bank of the river Cájula and passes an old mill, La Fábrica. You cross the river on stepping stones, pass a second mill then cross the river a further three times.

Climbing slightly the track reaches an ugly concrete-posted fence around an avocado grove. Careful! Here swing hard left on a small path which cuts through the riverside undergrowth. You should angle right across the river then climb up the left bank on a steep track.

Just 150 yards after crossing the river, at a point where the track narrows down, you come to an old carob tree. Here branch left onto a narrow mule track that zig-zags steeply uphill, crosses a water channel, passes more carob trees and then merges with a dirt track

The track leads up to a small farm where it swings right (**1 hr 20 mins**) and along a ridge from where there are good views of Canillas.

The road forks. Take the right fork. Still climbing you immediately pass a small house with blue railings then another with a round tower. You'll soon pass a farm with buttressed walls and high palm trees. The track meets with a paved road where you turn right down the hill.

After just 150 yards, branch off on a narrow track (cairn) that descends to the river. As you descend, you can see the track on the other side of the valley that you soon must follow, twisting its way up to Canillas.

You cross the river Cajula over a pretty old bridge, wind up to the road, turn right and, after just 25 yards, turn left onto the narrow path you could see earlier. The path leads you up towards Canillas.

When you come to a paved road, bear left, wind up to a green railing, and continue climbing. You enter the village along Calle La Plazoleta. Bearing right at the end, you reach the main square. Either Bar Romero or Restaurante La Plaza would make a good stop for refreshments. Remember that you now have a short, steep section of the walk to negotiate.

At the end of the square, climb Calle Hornos to house no13, where you swing left, then sharp right, and continue climbing. At the next fork, bear right. Then at the next junction, go left and carry on up Calle Canovas del Castillo. You come to another fork. Here take the right option and climb steeply towards an ugly breeze-block wall and soon you reach the Ermita de Santa Ana **(2 hrs)**.

Climb up to the ermita for great panoramic views - and a rest! When you leave the chapel, take the track that leads away from the main porch, back down to the tarmac road. Here you'll see two dirt tracks. Don't go left (signposted Zona Recreativa La Fábrica) but rather bear right and climb up towards an olive grove passing by a large water deposit to the left of the track

Continue on up the track and 10m after a second water deposit you reach a fork in the track. Here bear right, pass just to the left of a pylon, descend and then bear sharply left on a track which passes above a house with a swimming pool. It narrows to become a path which runs beside an irrigation channel. Stick to the main path which eventually meets with a new tarmac road. Turn right here and after 270m, at a cairn in front of an oleander bush, bear left and pick up the path which runs towards Cómpeta, through a beautiful swathe of irrigated terraces.

Eventually the path becomes a track and then meets with the road. Go right here, and then left, and retrace your footsteps along the Calle de San Antonio to the main square **(3 hrs)**

Distance:	12 km
Time Required:	5 / 5.5 hours
Rating:	Medium
Map:1:50000	Vélez-Málaga (1054) and Zafarraya (1040)

Cómpeta Circuit (via the Casa de la Mina)

The Walk of the Cool River

Though most of this itinerary follows dirt tracks rather than mountain, it is a memorable walk. Once you are up and over the Puerto de Collado, a stunning panorama opens out before you – a vast tract of virtually uninhabited Sierra stretching away to the north and east. It is amazing to consider that the crowded beaches of Nerja are little more than 10 miles distant. And after your steep climb up from Cómpeta, you are later rewarded with some shade when you pass by the Fábrica de la Luz., You may need to take boots and socks off to cross the river during the wetter months of the year and there are river pools for bathing. You have about 1km of asphalt road at the very end of the walk when you head back to Venta La Palma.

The Route

The walk begins just outside the Venta de Palma (you'll see it to your right, 1km from Cómpeta, on the road leading to Torrox).

Park outside the venta, then cross over the road and head up the dirt track. There are signs for Casa de la Mina and Finca Monte

Pino. Climb steeply up through the area known as Cruz de Monte, passing a number of satellite-dished villas.

You may meet the occasional Hamburg-plated 4-wheel-drive vehicle. Eventually you leave the villas behind and reach the pine forest. Soon the track arcs round to the right, and

here watch out for a red mark painted on a rock just to the left of the track.

Here cut left away from the track and climb steeply up beside a (dry) stream. The path at first follows its right hand bank. You pass an old calera (lime pit) on your right.

Follow the stream bed up this gulley until you meet with a scree slope that you follow along to the left. At the end of the scree, you'll see a water tank where the path swings sharp right and climbs, following the course marked by a painted arrow on the tank. Pass a quarry to your right and emerge onto the same track that you left earlier.

You are now at El Puerto del Collado. Turn left onto the track (not hard left leading up a very steep track) and follow signs for Casa de La Mina.

This is a beautiful section of the walk with wonderful views of the mountains of the Almijara Sierra.

Follow this track all the way to La Casa de la Mina, a white building clearly visible up ahead (the sandy-coloured building to the left is a hotel, completed five years ago but never opened). Just past Casa de la Mina **(1 hr 15 mins)**, branch sharp right off the track and drop down another good dirt track towards La Fábrica de la Luz.

The sparse vegetation here is due to a forest fire at the beginning of the 90s. Continue looping down and down (tempting short cuts are best avoided as they sometimes lead to a dead end), passing a house with arched windows and a cypress and eucalyptus grove just beneath it.

Just past the house, the track climbs slightly, then drops once again, passing a second farm with buildings to both sides of the track. Carry on down through the olive groves and, pass a sign for *zona de escalada* (marking an area of rock-climbing). There are views down to the Mediterranean from here.

Continue your descent. There are some fine old carob trees amongst the olives. Pass a house with an ugly, unrendered breeze-block wall, then drop down into the shade of the river bed where you come to the Fábrica de la Luz **(2 hrs 15 mins)**.

It is an agreeable spot with its palm and eucalyptus trees, running water and steep cliff face, and is certainly the first choice for a picnic.

You cross the (dry) river and then come to a fork. Don't turn left here for El Acebuchal (this track leads to Frigiliana) but rather go right, crossing the river once again.

Follow this track, climbing gently upwards, all the way to the Torrox/Competa road, with the river down to your left.

Eventually, after passing an electricity pylon and then Villa Carlota and Casa Cabra, you reach the main road. Here swing hard right, away from the road and climb up a track that soon leads you past Villa Damien. At the first fork in the road, by a palm tree, keep right, go past Casa Pastor, and at the second electricity pylon (it has a white base) turn left and climb a footpath running just to the left of three olive trees.

You again meet with the track that you should cross, continuing on your same course. This cuts off another large loop in the track. The dirt track winds on around the hillside between houses and villas until it reaches a fork where you take the right-hand option and climb towards a white water tank.

Soon your track merges with a rather better-surfaced one running more or less parallel with the road to Cómpeta, down to your left. Eventually this track drops down and meets the road. Bear right here and climb for about ten minutes along the tarmac back to Venta La Palma **(3 hrs 45 mins)**.

Cómpeta Circuit (via el Puerto Blanquillo)

Distance:	16 km
Time Required:	7.5/8 hours
Rating:	Medium/Difficult
Map: 1:50000	Zafarraya (1040)

The Walk of the High Axarquía

This long loop out from Cómpeta is a wonderful full-day walk. You have a tough climb at first. From Cómpeta to Puerto Blanquillo, there is a difference in height of almost 600m. But you could knock 200m off the ascent by getting a taxi to drop you by the football pitch above Cómpeta. The approach to Blanquillo is through wild and beautiful terrain and once you are over the top, the landscape suddenly changes as you drop down the beautiful Cueva del Melero valley. This long circuit could be shortened if you finish the walk in Canillas and return to Cómpeta by taxi. It takes in the very best of this part of the Almijara Sierra but because of the long initial climb you should get going early if you're walking this route in the warmer months. You could encounter lorries on the short section of dirt road that leads from the quarry down to Canillas de Albaida. The very best time to be walking this section would be between 2pm and 3pm when work stops for lunch.

The Route

The walk begins in the Plaza de la Almijara in Cómpeta. Leave the square at its top right-hand corner via a street that climbs steeply up to the shop El Rincón. Branch left here, climb up some steep steps, then swing right. Pass by a fountain to your right and, where this street begins to descend, turn left and carry on climbing. Take the higher option at any junction. When you reach a tarmac road, turn left,

pass the front of Bar El Loro and reach the Plaza del Carmen (just ask for la plaza if you get lost on the way up).

Here follow signs for the Campo de Fútbol. You meet with the road running around the top of the village. Go straight across here and continue up through an area that has been landscaped for a housing development (in 2000 the only building was the show house!).

From here there are fine views out to the Mediterranean. The concrete road ends and becomes a track that zigzags on up to the entrance of the spectacularly sited football pitch. Just before the entrance to the ground, go right and follow a sandy track along the right hand side of a fence. It becomes a path, climbs steeply, crosses a water pipe and meets with a track **(30 mins)**.

Here you turn right (there is a sign for the Parque Natural). Continue for just 20 yards past this

sign to a fork where you turn left onto a broad track that climbs gently upwards and soon reaches an area of pine plantation. You reach another junction by two metal posts where you swing right and continue climbing.

Looking ahead at this stage, you can see the road makes a huge loop left and you should be able to spot a path that cuts steeply up. Be ready to swing right here **(1hr)** onto a stony path that follows a line of pylons upwards.

The path merges with a track and continues steeply on up towards some pine trees. Now you begin to reap the rewards for this steep climb as the track levels and the views improve. Up ahead you'll now be able to see a fire observation post on top of a steep hill.

As you come to the base of this hill, the views open out eastwards. Carry on round the base of the hill, leaving the hut to your right, and descend slightly.

Careful! You must soon branch off away from the track onto a narrower path at the point where you see a rock with a red circle, just to the right of the track **(1 hr 45 mins)**.

The path soon passes an abandoned farm and then descends. There are red arrows/dots pointing your way. Pass by a *calera* (lime pit) and soon the path winds up to the entrance of a second ruined farmstead. An arrow directs you behind and to the left of the farm.

Pass a threshing circle and then red dots mark the continuation of the path. It runs beside a wall, climbs slightly, and soon arrives at a third ruined farm. The path passes by the farm and you begin to climb up the left-hand side of the Arroyo de Pradillos towards the top of the Puerto Blanquillo pass.

Red dots help guide you upwards. Keep your eyes on the left of the path. At the point just 10 yards before the path crosses the bed of the arroyo, bear left at a red dot and a cairn (they are easily missed). Now you follow cairns and red dots up to the top of Puerto Blanquillo **(2hrs 30 mins)** where the path runs up to meet with a broad track.

Here swing left onto the track and after 240m, at a cairn, turn right off the track and follow a loose, sandy path which zigzags steeply downhill. It soon improves and runs just to the left of a (dry) stream which it shortly crosses. The path then climbs for a short distance before dropping down and reaching the stream of the Arroyo de la Cueva del Melero. Ahead of you is a farmhouse.

Careful! Don't cross the stream here but rather bear sharply to the left, follow the left bank of the stream downwards for a short distance then cross over onto the terraces beneath the farm. Here the path runs along beside a fence, then drops downwards, sticking to the right bank of the river.

This is a beautiful section of the walk. Soon you see two more farm buildings. Pass through a ramshackle gate where the path forks. Don't swing left down towards a small wooden bridge but rather keep right (red dot), cross a (dry) stream, climb again and pass on between a large cork oak and a low wall.

The path drops down through the terraces and the gorge becomes more and more abrupt. Soon the path dips once more into the bed of the Arroyo de la Cueva del Melero, which it soon crosses. The path now becomes a track **(3 hrs 50 mins)** and you continue descending with the river down beneath you, to your right.

The track divides. Take the right fork downhill and after 150 metres, this track meets a fence. Here branch right off the track, then sharp left (red dot) and again you descend into the river valley along another gorgeous section of path cutting down through the terraces.

You arrive at the Fábrica de Luz de Canillas **(4 hrs 20 mins)** where you cross the river on a wooden bridge and follow a newly surfaced tarmac road down the left bank of the Rio Llanada de la Turvilla.

Pass a quarry as you continue down the valley on the main track. Lorries that come to fill up with gravel and sand often rumble by so ideally this part of the walk would be done between 2-4pm, when things slow down for lunch. Eventually you arrive at the Chapel of Ermita de Santa Ana **(5 hrs 05 mins)**.

Climb up for great views - and a rest! When you leave the chapel, retrace your footsteps away from the main porch, back down to the tarmac road. Here don't go left back towards La Fábrica but rather bear right and climb up towards an olive grove passing by a large water deposit to the left of the track.

Continue on up the track and 10m after a second

water deposit you reach a fork in the track. Here bear right, pass just to the left of a pylon, descend and then bear sharply left on a track which passes above a house with a swimming pool. It narrows to become a path which runs beside an irrigation channel. Stick to the main path which eventually meets with a new tarmac road. Turn right here and after 270m, at a cairn in front of an oleander bush, bear left and pick up the path which runs towards Competa, through a beautiful swathe of irrigated terraces.

Eventually the path becomes a track and then meets with the road. Go right here, and then left, and retrace your footsteps along the Calle de San Antonio to the main square **(6 hrs)**.

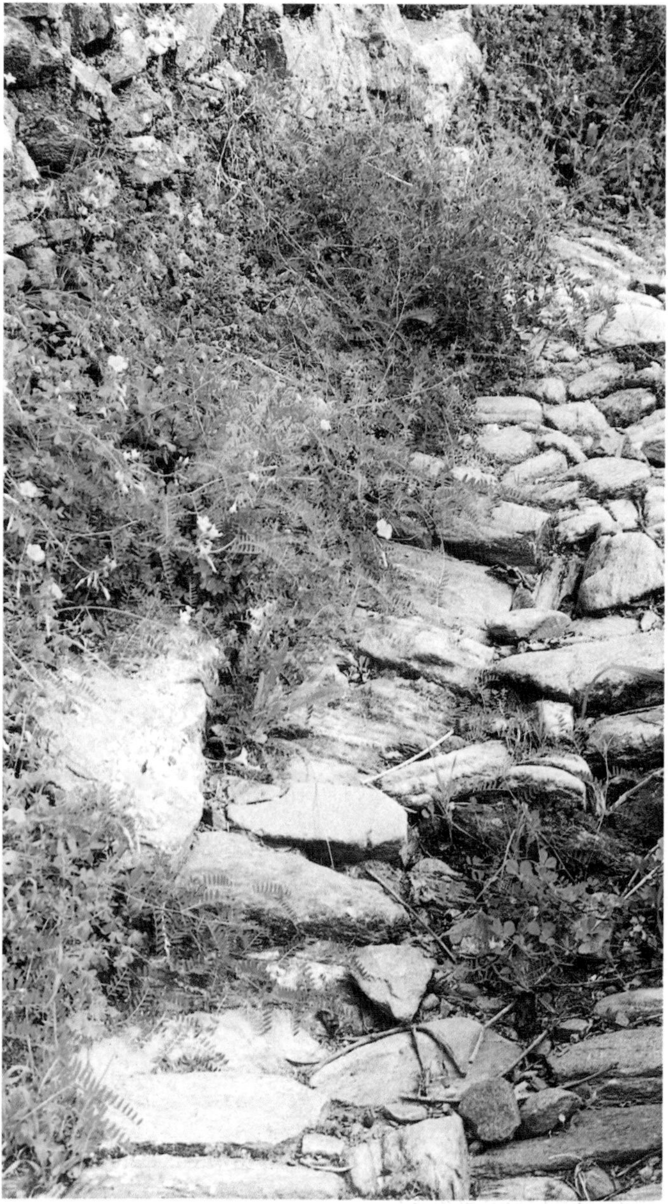

Canillas de Albaida Circuit

Distance:	11 km
Time Required:	4.5 / 5 hours
Rating:	Medium
Map: 1:50000	Zafarraya (1040)

The Walk of Stepping Stones and Mountain Chapels

One of my very favourite walks in La Axarquía which takes you out from Canillas de Albaida by way of an enchanting riverside path that meanders through thick stands of oleander, crossing back and forth across the Cájula river – easily passable unless there has been heavy rainfall. After a steep climb, the middle section of the walk takes you along dirt tracks and is quite different in feel. But it is easy to follow and there are fine views of the Sierra de Tejeda. The final section of the walk – there is a steep climb last thing – is along an ancient cobbled path with beautiful views of Canillas and the Chapel of Santa Ana. Try to do this when the oleander are in flower for a real spectacle. There are some prickly plants on the middle section before you reach the forestry track, so it's a good idea to take long trousers or gaiters along.

The Route

The walk begins from the car park at the entrance of the village as you come from Cómpeta. Head down the hill from the mini roundabout, passing the farmacia on the left and then the supermercado. At the bottom of the hill, bear left at a sign for Finca el Cerrillo, and drop steeply down the hill, passing by the chapel of San Antón to your left. Just past the chapel, bear right (don't go straight ahead to Árchez) and follow this road down to the river.

You pass some exceptionally lush vegetation as you descend. Cross the river and immediately bear sharp right on a concrete road towards an old mill. The road narrows to a path

following the course of the Cájula river, crossing its course a number of times. Pass a breeze-block building (20 mins) on your left and continue, now on the river's right bank.

You occasionally see red way-marking. Cross the river again and climb upwards. The path now becomes cobbled in places, and shortly you pass beneath an overhanging rock face before descending once again to the river. You cross the Cájula a couple more times before the path climbs up the river's left bank between two fences and becomes a track.

You'll see a white farmhouse up ahead of you but - careful! - branch right off this track (there is a small orange tree to the left of the track) at a sign for camino del río. Follow a narrow path that passes by a grove of young avocados. It winds, passes the stumps of a line of poplars and then continues on its rather serpentine course, occasionally marked by cairns. It is very pretty.

Shortly your path is crossed by another that has black nylon water pipes following its course. Here, turn right and then almost immediately left and wind down to the river. Cross over on the stepping stones.

The path then climbs up the other bank and soon becomes better defined (again you will see occasional red dots). The path divides and here bear left. A ruined house comes into sight on the other side of the river. Cross the river again and follow the path towards the house. Pass beneath the house, to its right, and then begin to climb steeply up the side of the valley. As you climb, you see a solitary modern building on the crown of a hill. Remember this landmark – you'll pass by it later in the walk.

The path swings right, descends, crosses a (dry) stream, then bears right again and winds uphill. You come to an area of terracing where you continue to climb. Up above you to your right, you soon spot a small farmhouse. Climb up to the farm. Your path passes just to its right before meeting a dirt track where you turn right **(1 hr 15 mins)**, now heading for the solitary building you saw earlier.

Just past this house, the track bears left and you continue towards the head of the Cájula gorge and a small cluster of houses. The track winds, descends and crosses el Arroyo de Luchina via a concrete bridge with rusting railings. It then climbs again. Down below are groves of olive and citrus. Pass a house on your right with a line of small pines to one side then, cross the river **(1 hr 45 mins)** and pass a row of poplars.

Continue on the main track (don't turn sharp right on a track leading down towards the river). Follow this track, climbing at first, on a course roughly parallel to the Cájula, back towards Canillas. You will eventually pass a water tank and then a house down to the right of the track with a solar panel

(2hrs). Just past this house, the track swings to the left and a track branches off right with a chain across it. Ignore this turning and continue for just 30 yards and then – careful! – turn right off the track onto a beautiful path (cobbled in parts) that zigzags all the way down to the river Llanada de Turvilla. Somewhere just off to one side of this path would make a memorable picnic spot.

Cross a bridge over the river and then bear right and wind up the other side of the valley towards the Santa Ana Chapel. Pass beneath the chapel – the gorge is now down to your right – and after a steep climb the path becomes a track that leads you just beneath the cemetery.

Here a green mesh fence runs to your right. Bear sharp left past house no.35, continue to the end of the street and then head up the hill past the supermercado and the bank to arrive back at your point of departure **(2hrs 45 mins)**.

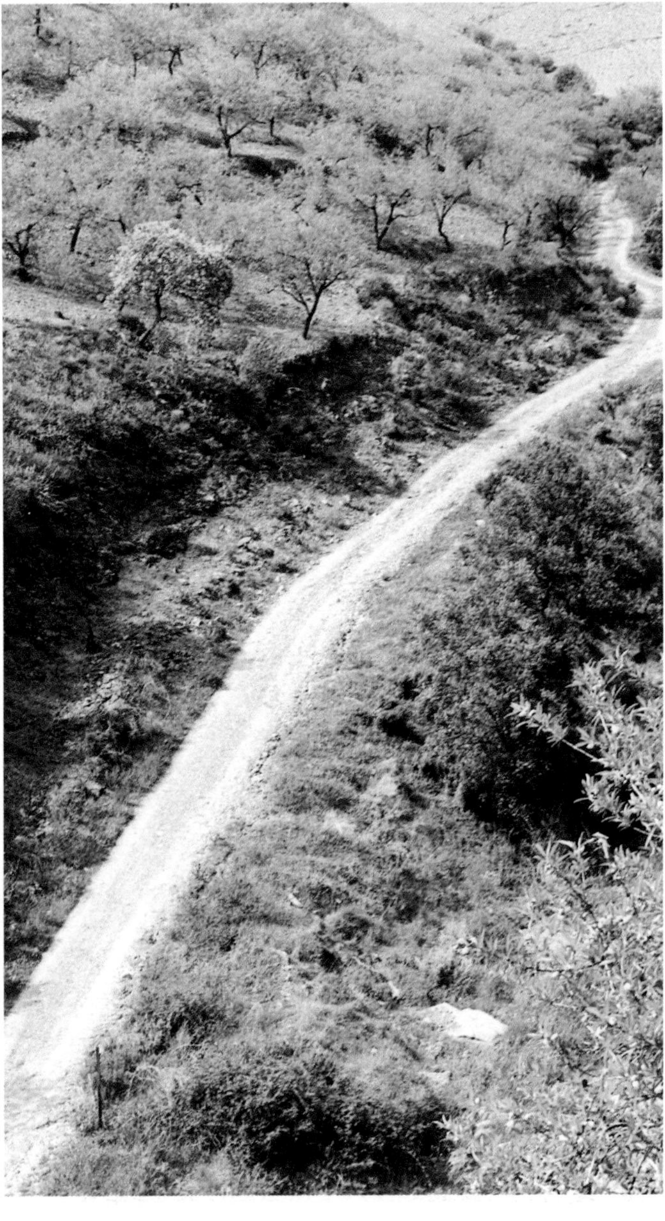

Distance.	17 km or 10 km
Time Required.	5.5/6 hours or 3.5/4 h
Rating.	Medium or Easy
Map: 1.50000	Vélez-Málaga (1054) and Zafarraya (1040)

The Walk
of the Moscatel Grape

This longish circuit skirts all the way round the Gúzman mountain (778m), just to the west of Archez. The walk is best undertaken when the vines are in leaf and is especially memorable during the grape harvest or in the autumn when the leaves change colour. In winter, the mountainside presents a much barer aspect but it still has a stark beauty and the views are always impressive. You could shorten this walk by about 1 hr 30 minutes by driving to the cutting on the Archez to Salares road, the highest point of the pass 2.5km from Archez. This saves you the climb up from the River Cájula past El Cerrillo. Nearly all the walk is along dirt tracks.

The Route.

The walk begins from the car park at the entrance of Canillas de Albaida as you arrive from Cómpeta.

Head downhill from the mini roundabout passing a farmacia to the left and then a supermercado. At the bottom of the hill, bear left at a sign for Finca el Cerrillo and drop steeply down the hill passing by the chapel of San Antón to your left. Just past the chapel, bear right (don't go straight ahead to Archez) and follow this road down to the river, past exceptionally lush vegetation.

Cross the river and climb steeply up a paved road. Soon you pass by El Cerrillo to your left. The road has now become a dirt track. There are fine views back to Canillas and down the Cájula valley to Archez. Continue on along this

track and arrive at the road leading from Archez to Salares (**40 mins**).

Turn left onto the road and, after just a few metres, go right at a sign for Los Eriales. Climb up through a deep cutting, at first on a tarmac surface and then on dirt track. After about 300 yards, the track divides and you bear sharply left and climb up past a solitary evergreen oak. Cómpeta and Canillas soon come into sight and the views improve.

There are vines to either side of the track. Pass by a farm on the right and continue along a high ridge. Soon you pick up a line of pylons and at the fourth pylon the track divides. Bear left and pass between two small farmsteads. Soon you pass a ruin with a modern house just to one side, down to your right (**1hr 20 mins**).

Stick to the main track that leads on between olive and almond groves. It climbs up towards a large shed on top of a hill and, shortly before you arrive at this building, is a point where five tracks meet. Here take the second track on the left that leads down and past a house with a small tower.

Remember that you will later be returning to this point to continue on back to Canillas. There is a difference in height between here and the village centre of nearly 350 feet. You could simply turn right here and shorten the walk by nearly an hour.

Drop down the hill to Corombela, where you arrive at the very top of the village. Pass by the school to your left and continue steeply down. Look for a low asbestos-roofed building opposite a tap. Turn right and drop down Calle Alta to a phone box where you bear left and soon arrive at the tiny village square (**2 hrs**).

Bar Cantero would be a nice spot for refreshments. After visiting the village, retrace your footsteps back up to the point where the five tracks meet. Don't take the track left that leads up to the large shed but go straight across and follow a track steeply down through olive and almond groves. The shed is now up to your left.

There are fantastic views over to the highest mountain of the Sierra de Tejeda, la Maroma (2069m). You are heading down towards a sharp bend of the Corombela to Daimalos road. The track descends and passes through a black gate (**2 hrs 25 mins**).

Cross a (dry) stream and then turn right onto a track that follows the left bank of the stream along a small valley that is planted with almonds and vines. At the first fork in the track, keep right, climbing, and at the next fork go left. Don't cross the stream where the wreckage of a car has been used to bridge the stream.

You now climb towards a solitary poplar and at the next fork go right and cross the stream. Soon you pass beneath the electricity

lines. Continue up on this track and soon, after passing a pylon, you'll come to a ruined farm. The views improve, the track passes right of the ruin, then levels and reaches another better surfaced track (**3 hrs**).

Turn right here. Follow this track, skirting round the western flank of the Guzman, back to the point where you earlier branched left after the cutting. Pass by this turning to your right. Ignore it and instead drop down through the cutting to the Archez-Salares road (**3 hrs 25 mins**).

Here you turn left onto the road and then next right at the sign for Canillas/Fogorate. Retrace your footsteps to the village (**4 hrs**).

Distance:	10 km
Time Required:	3.5/4 hours
Rating:	Easy/Medium
Map:1:50000	Vélez-Málaga (1054)

The Walk
of the Bountiful Valley

This easy half-day excursion links two attractive villages, Sayalonga and sleepy Corombela. The walk takes you down through the subtropical orchards of Sayalonga's terraced river valley where there is an astonishing variety of fruit trees. Then comes a steep climb up to Corombela passing by several small farmsteads and on the return leg there are excellent views of the Sierra de Tejeda and the Mediterrranean. Nearly all the walk is along tracks and this is a very easy circuit to follow. There is a short section of tarmac road when you leave Corombela, but there is very little traffic.

The Route

This walk begins in Sayalonga in the pretty Plaza Rafael Alcoba.

From here take the street that leads in front of the *ayuntamiento* into Calle Cristo and follow signs for the *cementerio redondo*. Branch right into Calle Rodríguez de la Fuente, then at the end of this narrow street turn left (unless you wish to visit the "round cemetery", the only one of its kind in Spain, in which case go right here and then retrace your footsteps). Pass the Santa Catalina church on your left, then bear right down the hill and come to a sign, marking the beginning of the walk to Corombela: 5 kms

You begin to descend, passing beneath the cemetery along a dirt track dropping down through fertile groves of fruit trees. Your route is occasionally

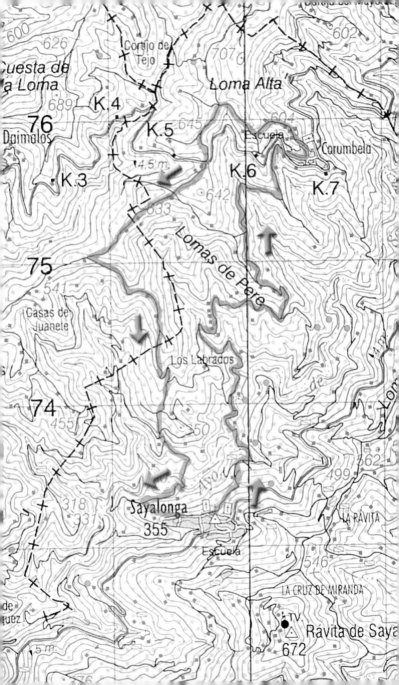

waymarked with white and yellow stripes. The track meets the river **(15 mins)**, runs along beside it for a short distance and then crosses over a narrow bridge.

Continue along with the river to your right and pass by the lovely Casa El Molino. It is possible to rent the whole place (see general introduction). The track climbs through more lush, well irrigated terraces. There are good views here back to Sayalonga.

Soon the track heads directly away from the river up a side valley, climbing steeply. Keep to the main track. Pass some stands of bamboo and then pass between a cluster of farm buildings. One of the farmhouses to the right has the *secaderos* (sun-drying patch) for the moscatel grapes.

Climbing on upwards, you soon pass by a second group of buildings to your left, some of which are being restored. You come to a fork in the track **(45 mins)**.

Don't turn right downhill towards an ugly rectangular goat shed but rather go left here and continue climbing. Competa is visible over to the right and soon Corombela comes into view. Keep to the main track. You pass by several small farms. The track descends slightly **(1 hr)**, passes over a gulley and then passes Las Tres Fuentes (the Three Springs) on your left.

Continue to wind on up towards Corombela. Pass the town football pitch and the track comes up to meet a tarmac road. Go straight across the road into Corombela **(1 hr 20 mins)**.

Bear left just past the bakery and you'll arrive at Bar Cantero, a good place for a cool drink after the long climb from Sayalonga. Here swing left, past the Covirán supermarket, into calle Las Pitas.

Continue past a garishly painted building to your right and head along a track that runs just above the Corombela/ Daimalos road, passing through groves of almonds, olives and loquats. The track climbs, passes Villa Alminara, then drops down past a ruin and meets the tarmac road that you must now follow up to the top of the pass. After ten minutes of asphalt-bashing, at a point where the road swings sharply right, you turn left onto a track **(1 hr 45 mins)**.

The track immediately passes by a farm (you can buy wine here) with *secaderos* for the grapes. You reach a first fork, from where there are views down to the sea. Here fork right and soon you pass above four small farms. Follow a ridge along and then drop down past a rather ugly breeze-block building. You will now see a modern house with arches up ahead of you.

On a clear day, across to your right, there are splendid views of the Sierra de Tejeda and its highest point, La Maroma (2069m). Just before you reach the house with the arches, swing left onto a track that runs steeply downhill. You can see Sayalonga on the other side of the valley. Pass two pretty farms and then pass by a little ruin on the right (a possible picnic spot and there is shade beneath a huge carob just beneath it to the right).

Keep to the main track. It descends, swings sharply left and then right again, still dropping down. You now see a ruined farm ahead of you on a ridge. The track winds round and just before you reach the ruin you should branch right, away from the track.

Pass just a few yards to the right of the ruin and then bear sharp right and drop down onto a rough track that zigzags down the hill towards a house with two palm trees. It meets a better track. Follow it to the right, down to the palm-trees and the farm. Here you turn left and continue your descent, passing a water tank and fertile groves of fruit trees before you reach the river **(2 hrs 15 mins)**.

Cross over the river (you may need to take boots and socks off in the wetter months) and bear right and follow a concreted road steeply uphill. Shortly after passing a pylon you come to a white building to the left of the track; the smell lets you know that its inhabitants are pigs. Immediately before this building branch left and climb steeply on a path which runs between two fences. It soon widens and meets with a concreted section of track. At the end of this bear left and then right to reach the first houses in the village. Head along to the end of Calle Loma then turn left into Calle Campillos. Pass a chemists ('farmacia') then bear right and in front of house number 17 bear right again into Calle Nueva to reach Plaza de Andalucía. Here turn left into Calle Piaggine (named after the village's twin town) and at the end of this street climb a steep flight of steps to arrive back in Plaza Rafael Alcoba **(2 hrs 40 mins)**.

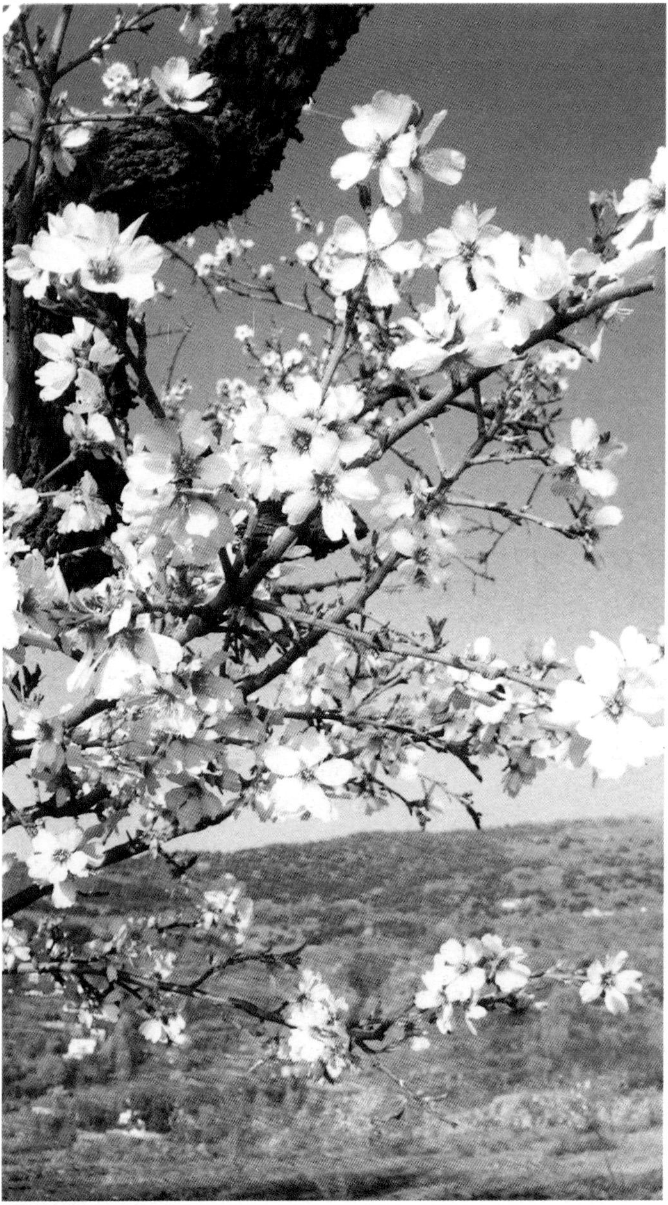

THE ALPUJARRAS

The area

The Alpujarras are a series of high villages that cling to the southern flank of the Sierra Nevada and face out across the Mediterranean to the Atlas mountains of Morocco. The area surrounding these villages is encompassed within the Parque Natural de La Sierra Nevada, that was created in 1989 and covers an area of 171,0000 hectares.

As well as the Alpujarras, it includes mainland Spain's most lofty peaks, the highest of them being the mighty Mulhacén, rising to 3481 metres. The area's great natural beauty and its huge biological and geomorphological diversity has meant that since the mid- eighties the Sierra Nevada has been one of UNESCO's Biosphere Reserves. And the higher area of the Park has just recently been upgraded to *Parque Nacional* status.

The life-giver of the mountain range is the melt-water that runs down off the high Sierra for nearly the whole of the year. Over the course of the centuries, it has cut a series of deep river valleys or *barrancos* (see glossary) that radiate out from the central Sierra .

Since the arrival of the Moors in the Middle Ages, a number of meticulously crafted *acequias* or irrigation channels have brought this same water to the carefully tended terraces that have been cut out of the hillsides surrounding the villages. To see these swathes of richly cultivated land in this otherwise harsh, often barren landscape, is like coming across an oasis in the desert.

It is no wonder that the Moors were loathe to leave these villages and lingered on for almost a century after the fall of Granada. They were abandoning a truly monumental feat of engineering. It wasn't until 1568 and the last desperate Morisco uprisings that they finally gave up the land for lost, accepted their defeat and limped across the Strait back to Africa.

The villages they left behind still have an unmistakably north-African feel with their flat-roofed, whitewashed houses huddling tightly together on the steep hillsides. One of their most striking features are the covered passageways or *tinaos* that often span the narrow streets forming both a porch and a platform for a room above. The *tinaos* seem to bind the villages together and occasionally form narrow tunnels between the houses, conveying a distinctly soukh-like feel.

Times have changed since a young Gerard Brennan found in the Alpujarras a remote, undiscovered corner of Europe. For the past twenty years, Bubión, Trevélez and the villages at the western end of the Sierra have become a popular weekend resort with the Spaniards. Thanks to the arrival of more and more visitors, there are numerous hotels and hostals - and good restaurants, too. The downside of this sudden increase in tourism is that the character of some of the villages is beginning to change. There are more souvenir shops, pub-style bars and Spanish rather than Alpujarran cuisine in the restaurants. The legendary *tapas* (so big that they can be a meal in themselves) are disappearing.

The area has also begun to attract growing number of New Age travellers from the North of Europe. As well as the impromptu camps of VW and Bedford vans you come across in and around Orgiva, there is a more established, alternative community. Yoga, Zen-Buddhism, aromatherapy, permaculture and creative workshops are all now a part of life in the Sierra, along with goat-herding and cheese-making. Get hold of a copy of Chris Stewart's *Driving Over Lemons* for a tender and entertaining account of moving into this area in search of the Good Life.

And walkers have arrived, too. Many come to climb the higher peaks or to undertake higher traverses of the Sierra. There is a good system of mountain refuges and more are on the way. The routes described in this chapter stick to a lower network of foot paths that, with the exception of the Walk of the Seven Lagoons, are easier day and half-day walks.

Thanks to the isolation of the Alpujarra, and the comparatively recent arrival of paved roads, the footpaths linking the villages are mostly intact and they make for wonderful walking. Most routes described have at least one steep climb (there is no such thing as a gentle *barranco* – see glossary), but the walking is varied and often spectacular.

Because of the height of the villages – most of these walks start from a height of about 1000 metres – you can still walk comfortably in the Alpujarras in June and September, although during these months you should start out early. During the winter months, the snow rarely settles for long below 1200m, and this can be a wonderful time to visit, especially when the almond trees are in blossom. Spring is a double treat, when the flowers are at their best and temperatures mild enough for lazy picnics along the way.

Other Walks

The GR7. This long-distance route, running all the way from Andorra to Algeciras, cuts across the middle of the Alpujarras (the walk described from Bérchules to Júviles follows a part of this route). You could easily follow the GR7 from village to village for five or six days, but you will need maps because the way marking is sometimes confusing).

Eastern Alpujarra. There is also good walking at the eastern end of the Alpujarras. A good base here is Casa de Las Chimeneas in Mairena, owned by a young British couple, David & Emma Illsley (Tel 958 76 03 52).

Southern Alpujarra. There are a number of lower walks out from the Alquería de Morayma (Tel 958 34 32 21), a beautiful small inn close to Cádiar. The owner, Mariano, has a number of route descriptions.

Shorter Routes. Elma Thompson's leaflets *Exploring the Alpujarras* describe a series of more gentle walks, most of them radiating out from Bubión and Poqueira.

Longer Routes. The Lonely Planet guide *Trekking in Spain* describes the high traverse of the Sierra Nevada (you need to camp) as well as the route up to the Mulhacén.

Maps.

The most detailed maps available of the area are the 1:25000 series of the Instituto Geográfico Nacional, but you will need several of them to cover the walks listed here. It is probably best to stick with the Instituto Geográfico Nacional's 1:50000 map (mapa/guía)- Sierra Nevada. If you choose to go for the individual 1:50000 series, you will need nos. 1027, 1042 and 1043. Trevélez falls right on the border of two maps, 1027 and 1042, but 95% of the two routes that leave from the village are covered by the 1027 map (Güéjar-Sierra). Alpina's 1:40000 map Sierra Nevada/La Alpujarra is also a possibility although I have found that occasionally tracks are missing from the map.

The best place to pick up maps and guide books to the area is in the Centro de Visitantes in Pampaneira, where the excellent Nevadense guides are based. The amount of assembled literature and maps are really impressive (some of it in English, too). You should pass by here at the beginning of any visit. It is, conveniently, in one of the first villages you pass through coming from the west.

Best Places to Sleep

Ferreirola

Sierra y Mar.

Tel: 958 766 171
Fax: 958 857 367
A delightful guesthouse in a tiny, unspoiled village. Always a first choice but because of its popularity it is often fully booked. Owners José and Inge have exceptional knowledge of walks and the area. Approx. 45 euros. (Taxi: José Luis y Paco 958 76 60 05). **Best eats**: Restaurante El Aljibe in the village.

Village Houses.

If Sierra y Mar is full, there are rooms and apartments to rent in the village from Fernando of Nevadense. Tel 958 76 62 53 (Taxi: see above).

Bérchules

Hotel Los Bérchules.

Tel: 958 852 530
Fax: 958 769 000
Very comfortable small hotel on outskirts of village, a perfect base for the Bérchules circuit. English owner Wendy is exceptionally kind and helpful. Good views out across the valley. Approx. 40 euros. (Taxi: Wendy can arrange any transfers). **Best eats**: here or Bar La Triana in the village.

Trevélez

Hotel La Fragua.

Tel: 958 858 626
Fax: 958 858 614.
A fairly basic, small hotel at the top of the village with an excellent restaurant just a few yards away. Popular with walking groups from the UK. 35 euros. (Taxi: José Luis 958 85 87 27 or 609 91 16 57). **Best Eats**: here.

Bubión

Las Terrazas.

Tel: 958 763 252
Fax: 958 763 034.
Simple accommodation and friendly owners. Good value. Mountain bikes available. Approx. 30 euros. (Taxi José 958 76 30 25). **Best Eats**: Restaurante Teide.

Capileira

Finca Los Llanos.

Tel: 958 763 071
A nice quiet place with pool, at the top of the village off to the side of road to Sierra Nevada. Approx. 60 euros. (Taxi: hotel can arrange all transfers). **Best Eats**: Restaurante El Tilo (good place to try the famous *plato alpujarreño*).

Distance:	8km
Time Required:	3.5/4 hours
Rating:	Medium
Map:1:50000	Sierra Nevada General Map or Lanjarón (1042)

The Walk of the Ruined Mills & the Arab Baths

This walk begins and ends in the tiny village of Ferreirola. For most of the way, it follows old muleteer tracks that twice cross the steep-sided barranco of the Río Trevélez. Although there are two steep uphill sections, this is an easy half-day walk that you could stretch out by picnicking somewhere along the way – or by stopping for a coffee in Busquístar. This itinerary has a kilometre or so of road-walking but there is virtually no traffic and the views are excellent. José and Inge, the owners of the delightful Sierra and Mar guest house in Ferreirola (the obvious first choice if you are plan to overnight here) kindly shared this route with me. Ferreirola and Busquístar are not in the least bit touristy and this would be a lovely first walk in the Alpujarras

The Route

Your walk begins in the main square of Ferreirola in front of the church.

Pass in front of the four fountains and continue past Villa Kiko and then descend between two stone walls. Here you pick up red and white GR route marking. The street narrows, doglegs right and then left and you pass beneath a *tinao* (glossary). Pass a newly built section of high wall on your left and then pick up a path leading out from the village.

Pass by a spring, and then a second one, both just to the left of the path. The path bears right, crosses a bridge then traverses a rocky area just beyond which a path forks left. Ignore this and after

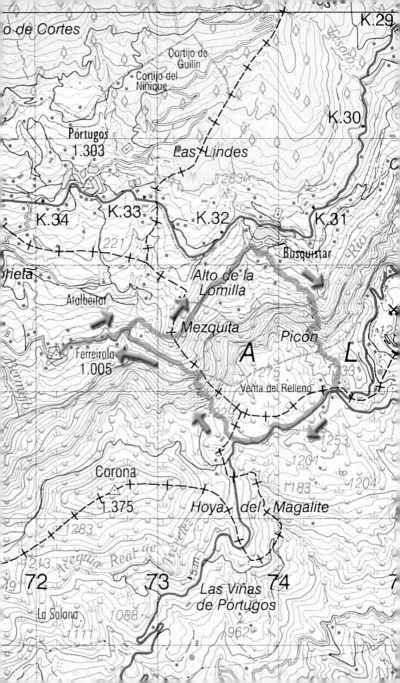

just 60m, at a second fork and a sign for 'Busquístar', branch left and climb gently upwards.

The path divides again. Fork left and soon you reach a track. Here bear right and descend slightly through an area of terraced fields beneath Busquístar. You reach a stand of poplars. Here carry on uphill and then cross a bridge. The path becomes still steeper and you arrive **(45 mins)** at the outskirts of the village.

You'll see a sign for Camino a Ferreirola. Here, if you are planning to visit the village, turn left and climb up into the village, but remember that later you will need to retrace your footsteps back to this sign. This path leads up past Casa de Las Lillas where you could have an early lunch (open 1-4pm). If you're not planning to visit the village, at the Camino a Ferreirola sign turn right down the hill and then go left at a door with a painted arrow pointing your way.

Continue skirting round the bottom of the village until you reach a sign for Camino del Río. Go right here and drop steeply down through the terraces. Soon you need to bear left round a house with a horseshoe above its entrance.

As you drop down to the river, you'll see wooden posts and red dots marking your way. A footbridge leads you across the river by a ruined mill (1 hr) and the path now zigzags steeply up the other side of the gorge. Prepare yourself for a long, steep climb! The path eventually levels and meets with a tarmac road **(1 hr 35 mins)** just to the left of the Venta de Relleno.

Turn right onto the road in the direction of Almegíjar/Torvizcón. You should continue until you see a group of 5 buildings **(1 hr 50 mins)** just to the right of the road. Turn right off the road at a marker post and climb up towards these buildings, watching out for a second marker post just to the right of the track. Here

turn right, away from the track, and drop back down towards the River Trevélez.

After 5 minutes or so of descending, the path runs just to the left of the overgrown ruin of some Arab baths.

There is little to see now. Ferreirola is clearly visible on the other side of the valley. As you descend you'll occasionally spot marker posts. You cross the river once again, swing left in front of a second ruined mill **(2 hrs 20 mins)** and climb up the northern side of the *barranco*.

You reach the fork where earlier in the walk you took the higher option to Busquístar. Here bear left and return to Ferreirola and retrace the path that you followed earlier in the day, all the way back to the square in front of the church **(3hrs)**.

Capileira Circuit

Distance:	9 km
Time Required:	4/4.5 hours
Rating:	Medium
Map: 1:50000	Sierra Nevada General Map or Lanjarón (1042)

The Walk
of the High Alpujarra

This loop walk begins and ends in the pretty village of Capileira and takes you up to the generating station of La Cebadilla. Although your destination is at a height of over 1600m, you are departing from one of the highest villages in the Alpujarras (1432m) - so there is not too much climbing on this route. The views down the Poqueira river valley are exceptional and there is the possibility of extending this walk (see below) from a point above La Cebadilla. Most of the walk follows old footpaths that cut across the old terracing of the valley. There is also a half-hour stretch of track on the return leg before you pick up the loveliest of paths that drops steeply down to Capileira.

The Route

The walk begins at the *ayuntamiento* (town hall) of Capileira. You see it on your right as you come from Bubión.

Cross the road and take the street leading into the village by a phone box. Turn left at restaurant El Tilo, then turn right and pass in front of its close relative, Bar El Tilo. At the end of this small square you enter Calle del Cubo,

drop down and then bear right in front of Apartamentos Vista Veleta.

Continue along this paved road following a line of black street lamps. Passing by two '*eras*' (glossary) the road becomes a stony track and descends. It passes a water tank to the left of the path, then a spring. Soon you reach a wooden marker post with a black and red dot, just to the right of the path **(15 mins)**.

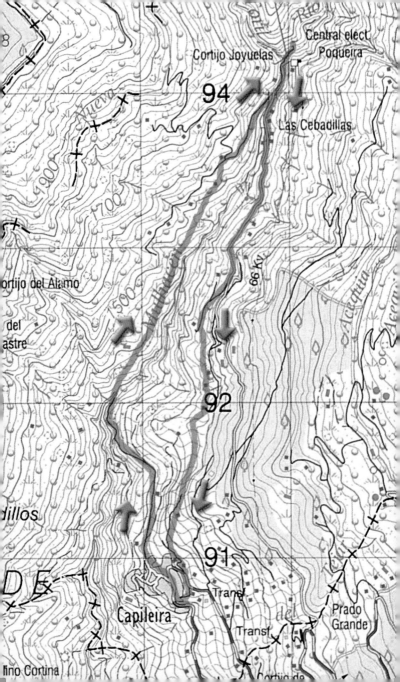

Here swing hard left and begin to descend more steeply.

Keep to the main path, ignoring a fork left. You pass beneath a stone hut, reach the river, then cross a bridge by a sign '*aguas de alta montaña*'. The path swings right, climbs and after 50m a section of wooden barrier runs to the right of the path.

Don't swing left on a path that leads up to a threshing circle. Continue on a course roughly parallel to the river, climbing gradually up across the terracing. Pass a section where the path has been damaged by heavy rains – but it soon improves.

Don't worry about the lack of marker posts on this section. They eventually reappear but are best forgotten on this walk to avoid confusion. Pass by a ruined farmstead with a threshing circle. The path still runs more or less parallel to the river, occasionally looping up to a higher level. The path

swings left **(40 mins)** in front of the wall of a terrace then swings right again and continues climbing.

Pass by a row of poplars and then a renovated farm building to your left. The path begins to loop sharply up. Look for a transmitter mast up ahead. You will later pass it by. The path bears left when it reaches a small *barranco* (gorge) and then crosses it a little higher up.

Soon a ramshackle fence runs to the right of the path and leads you up to a farm with solar panels and barking dogs **(1 hr)**.

Pass to the left of the farm and drop down for just a short distance. Cross a small bridge and after 100m you come to a fork where you branch left and climb. Crossing a terrace, you soon pass another tumbledown farm. You come to another line of poplars where you swing left and follow the line of the trees upwards. You pass a threshing circle, climb more steeply, then pass one more stone build-ing to your left before arriving at the transmitter mast **(1hr 15mins)**.

Just to its right is an ugly modern building with a bridge leading to its front door. A few yards past this bridge, turn right and wind downhill on a path that soon picks up a wide track leading down to the river and the H.E.P. buildings. You come to the bridge crossing the River Poqueira **(1hr 30 mins)**.

Here you have a choice. You could extend this circuit by carrying on up the track by the river to see the power station. Above it, the original millrace has been replaced by a snaking pipe. It looks almost surreal up against the shaley side of the barranco. If you continue on up the track and cross a second, higher bridge you'll reach a sign marking various higher circuits up the Poqueira river valley towards Las Tomas.

You could do a short up-and-down walk here to find

a good picnic spot. Other-wise retrace your footsteps to the bridge **(2 hrs)** below the generating station, cross over and then swing right past the buildings where the workers of the station once lived.

The track climbs gradu-ally upwards, heading south back towards Capileira. Ignore a track that branches off right to Cortijo Roble, but be ready to branch right approxi-mately 100 metres after you pass beneath the electricity lines **(2hrs 20 mins)**.

Drop down, pass by a house and you will see a second, slate-built house up ahead. A water channel soon runs to the left of your path. Pass a threshing circle. The path now follows the fence of this second house before it climbs and runs along just beneath a pine plantation. Continue past a large water tank on this same course towards Capileira. Don't swing downhill to the right at a first marker post!

You soon will reach a second fork in the path. Turn right and go down past two small huts. You come to the outskirts of the village. At the first house, bear right, drop down Calle Castillo, head straight across at the next crossroads and you'll emerge at the telephone box next to restaurant El Tilo. Here you turn left and retrace your footsteps back to the town hall **(3 hrs)**.

Distance:	14 km
Time Required:	4.5 / 5 hours
Rating:	Medium
Map: 1:50000	Sierra Nevada General Map or Lanjarón (1042) and Güéjar-Sierra (1027)

The Walk of Rock, Ravine and 'Rascavieja'

This could be a good first walk out from Trevélez. Although you cover almost 14km, there is little in the way of steep climbing. The first half of the loop takes you along the eastern bank of the river Trevélez. On the higher sections there are wonderful views across to the Mulhacén and the Alcazaba peaks. You then drop down into the river valley where you follow a beautiful riverside path all the way back to the village. Some sections of this route are slightly overgrown and there is one looser section of path when you drop down into the barranco of the river Trevélez. You'll see lots of rascavieja (adenocarpus) on this walk, the bushy plant that so typifies this part of the Alpujarra. Its rich yellow flowers are a magnificent sight when they flower in April/May.

The Route

The walk begins in front of Restaurante González in Plaza Francisco Abellán at the bottom of the village.

Cross the square and just behind the fountain turn right and climb up Calle Ladeira. At a wash house with a Virgin, bear right. The street soon becomes a track. After just

100 metres, it swings left, passes behind a white building, narrows down and then crosses a (dry) stream bed.

The path drops, crosses a second (dry) stream and then meets a dirt track. Bear right and follow the track down to the river you cross via a newly-built bridge. The track climbs and passes a farm. Just

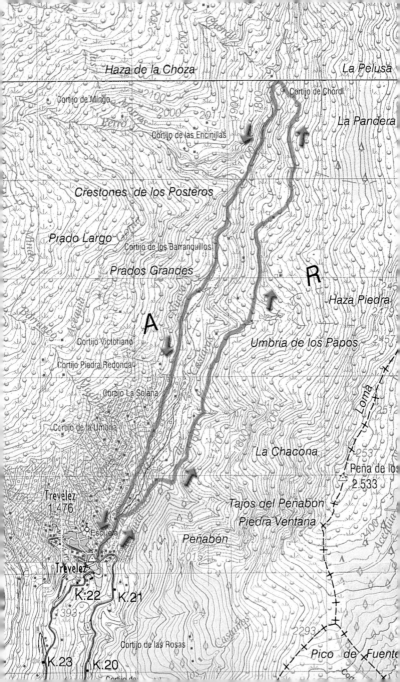

forty metres past the farm, cut left away from the track onto a path that climbs, goes through a gap in a fence, and then passes by a cattle pen.

The path runs roughly parallel to the River Trevélez, down below you to the left. Pass a threshing circle, an abandoned farm and then a small outbuilding without a roof before crossing a wide *acequia* (irrigation channel). Soon the path loops upwards before resuming its course. It narrows and shortly passes to the right of a ruined farmstead with an *era* (threshing area) **(35 mins)**.

The path, after traversing the mountainside soon crosses another steep-sided barranco. Continue on past another farm to your left. It has solar panels on the roof. Climb gently on up and come to a point where the path divides. Take the more pronounced right fork and climb up towards a stone building. Soon the path drops into another *barranco*, crosses a (dry) stream, goes through a

fence and shortly crosses a second (dry) stream. Now follow the course of an *acequia* before climbing once again, now on a rather looser path. It soon levels and then passes just above a threshing circle before climbing indistinctly up towards a holly oak. The path winds, passes over some rocks, then climbs up to a farm house **(1hr 5 mins)**.

Pass immediately to the left of the building and about half way up the farm's side-wall, bear left onto an indistinct path that arcs away from the farm. It soon improves. At this point in the walk, there are lovely views out across the river valley.

The path begins to descend through thick stands of *rascavieja*. Pass a ruined building to your left. Stick to the main path and don't be tempted to swing down to the left. Soon it zigzags steeply up, passes by an impressive rocky outcrop and then goes through a wire-and-post gate. You now come to post gate. You now come to an area of terracing and the path passes just behind a solitary farm. Here the path swings right, climbs and passes behind an overgrown ruin.

Soon you have a (dry) *acequia* to your left. Go through a fence and then resume a similar course through scrubby vegetation before passing between two farm buildings. Cross an *acequia*. The path climbs up over rather loose, shaley ground. There are fantastic views across the valley towards the Mulhacén.

The path levels and then runs parallel to another *acequia*. Careful! You reach a point where this water channel becomes overgrown and the path divides.

Don't climb up the hill (into a clump of dog rose!) but rather swing left (you may see a small cairn) and head down towards the river on a path whose first part has been quite badly churned up by cattle. It

soon improves. Dip down and then up again, past a rocky outcrop. The path goes through a gate in a fence, then winds down through thicker undergrowth, crosses a *barranco*, and then drops down over looser terrain to a farm with solar panels called El Cortijo del Chordi **(2 hrs)**.

At the farm swing left, pass just to the right of the threshing floor and pick up a good path looping down to the river. Here you bear left on a well-defined path that hugs the left bank. This could be a good spot for a picnic.

After a while, the path runs in closer to the river and you reach a bridge. Don't cross it but rather continue down the left bank until you come to a second bridge. Cross over and continue down the right bank of the river, just beneath the Acequia Nueva.

The valley widens, you go through a gate, and soon there is a fence between you and the river. The path is now cobbled in parts.

Climb slightly away from the river, cross a (dry) stream bed and Trevélez comes into sight. Shortly you'll see the bridge you crossed at the beginning of your walk. Don't drop down to it but keep higher, sticking to your same course, and soon you'll meet with the track leading back up to the village. You could retrace your steps by swinging left onto the path you followed earlier in the day or, for a change, follow the track up to the top end of the village **(3 hrs 45 mins)** before returning to the start point.

Distance:	14.5 km
Time Required:	7.5/8 hours
Rating:	Medium/Difficult
Maps: 1:50000	Sierra Nevada General Map or Lanjarón (1042) and Güéjar-Sierra (1027)

Trevélez
High Circuit

The Walk
of the Seven Lagoons

This long full-day walk takes you up to the beautiful high cirque (2900m) which lies just beneath mainland Spain's highest peak, the Mulhacén (3479m). From Trevélez you have a climb of nearly 1500m ,so to enjoy this circuit you should be reasonably fit and set out early. You can shorten the walk by almost 3 hours/6 km by ending the climb at the ruins of Cortijo La Campiñuela. In the colder months there is often snow on the higher sections of the walk, so check before leaving Trevélez. The path followed on the circular option from La Campiñuela is steep and loose at times. If in doubt you can simply make this an up-and-down walk for as far as the mood takes you.

The Route

Begin at the square at the bottom of the village in front of bar Rosales. Go up the hill following signs for Mesón La Fragua. Here bear sharp left, pass Hotel La Fragua and then turn right beneath an archway (tinao). On the other side of the arch, turn right into Calle Horno, pass by an old wash house and after just 40m, at a yellow arrow on a telegraph pole, turn left.

A narrow cobbled path leads up through the terraces. The Río Trevélez is down to your right. Soon your path merges with a second, better-defined one, and shortly crosses a small stone bridge. You'll see yellow waymarking. Cross a (dry) stream and continue to climb, passing a small white building and then crossing a second small bridge. The path divides (**20 mins**). Here carry straight on. You'll see

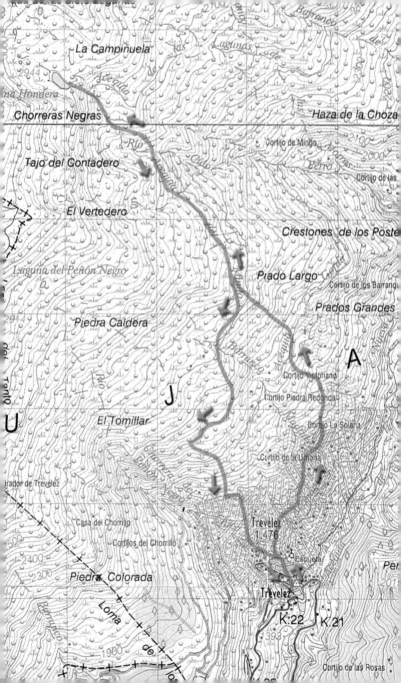

red and white marker posts. Pass a farm with solar panels (and dogs), then cross another (dry) stream. Pass by a threshing platform and, about 200 metres further on, the path divides. Bear left and climb. Soon a rock with a white arrow indicates the course to follow. Look for red and white waymarking.

Careful! At a small cairn **(45 mins)**, bear left onto a smaller path. Red dots mark the way. The path bears left, then meets with a fence. Here go through a wire-and-post gate and continue climbing steeply. Cairns guide you across this rather looser terrain. Soon a flimsy fence runs to your left. Trevélez is visible way down beneath you.

After a longish climb, the path swings right and runs more or less parallel to the Trevélez gorge, just beneath a water channel (*Acequia Gorda*) and a fence. You reach another fence. Go through a wire-and-post gate and shortly afterwards you cross the water channel, just past two wooden posts. Follow the left bank of the channel along for about 200 yards, then bear left and pass through a gap in a fence.

You now climb steeply through an area of young pines. You lose the red dots but the path is clear and soon you see cairns marking your way. The trees thin out and the path zigzags steeply up through the shale to another fence, where you go through another wire-and-post gate (sometimes open), then follow the fence along.

The fence ends and you climb up towards a low wall. It lies between you and the rocky massif of the Mulhacén. The path swings right, crosses a water channel (Acequia del Mundo) and red dots again mark your way. You reach a flat area where there is a ruined farm, Cortijo la Campiñuela **(2 hrs 15 mins)**. The path swings to the right, passes beween the farm and a threshing circle, climbs up past a tumbledown corral and then divides. Bear left here and continue climbing over rather looser, shaley ground. Cairns and occasional red dots help to guide you up. Soon you have a *barranco* down to your right. The path eventually winds down and crosses the Río Culo de Perro at a point where the banks of the stream have been shored up with concrete.

Once across the (dry) river, bear left. Don't head straight across towards a cairn. The path becomes indistinct but after running parallel to the river bank for a short distance you pick up cairns. The path bears slightly to the right, away from the stream, and climbs.

After approximately 15 minutes, the path divides. Bear left and climb up the river Culo de Perro's steep, rocky right bank (marked on some maps as Chorreras Negras – literally 'the small, dark waterfalls' - you'll see why). Cross the rocky river bed just before the top of the ridge and reach the beautiful glacial cirque of Siete

Lagunas **(3 hrs 45 mins)**. It lies between Alcazaba (3360m) and Mulhacén (3478m), both of which can be climbed from here. But this walk finishes here, at 2900m, on the wonderful flat, grassy area between the Siete Lagunas (seven tarns). A perfect picnic spot.

You now have a choice. The easiest option is simply to retrace your footsteps all the way back to Trevélez **(6 hrs 15 mins)**. A slightly more difficult option is to first return to the ruins of Cortijo La Campiñuela **(4 hrs 45 mins)**. Bear right from the ruin onto a good path that descends through very old terracing and meets and then then crosses the Acequia del Mundo.

Follow it along and then cross once again to its upper bank. Trevélez comes into view. Shortly afterwards a fence runs to your left and then your path (and the fence, too) drops sharply into the Barranco Madrid. Cross it just 20 yards up from the fence. The path narrows and shortly afterwards divides.

Branch left and pick up cairns that guide you down a looser-surfaced path. Go through a fence, descend to a flatter area and here, where you reach another fence, go right (don't go through the gap). The path runs indistinctly along, just to the right of the fence, then drops down to another flat area where it passes beneath a small dry-stone hut. You pass another tumbledown building to your right and continue on down.

The path occasionally divides but there are cairns to help. At a grassy area, you bear left and the path again becomes looser underfoot as it drops down to the left of a barbed wire fence, then passes through a wire-and-post gate. Cairns still mark the way. The path narrows to little more than a goat's track before it contours right (slightly away from Trevélez) towards an isolated farm. Just before the farm (**5 hrs 45 mins**), you swing hard left and drop down through the terraces east of the farm.

This section is more difficult to follow but you are soon heading towards a stone platform perched high at the end of the ridge up ahead of you. Heading for this, you meet a *barranco*, where you bear right and follow on down on its right bank.

The path winds round and then reaches a gate. On the other side of the gate you pick up a much clearer path that runs beneath a stone wall, then crosses the bottom of the barranco. Continue on down, cross a water channel and then bear right, still descending. The path becomes cobbled in parts, passes a threshing circle and drops down a (dry) gulley. Pass another threshing circle perched high to your right and reach another water channel. Here swing left and follow the narrow bank of the channel until you see an ugly breeze block building to your left. Turn right here and descend to meet the path you followed earlier in the day. It leads you back to Hotel La Fragua (**6 hrs 15 mins**).

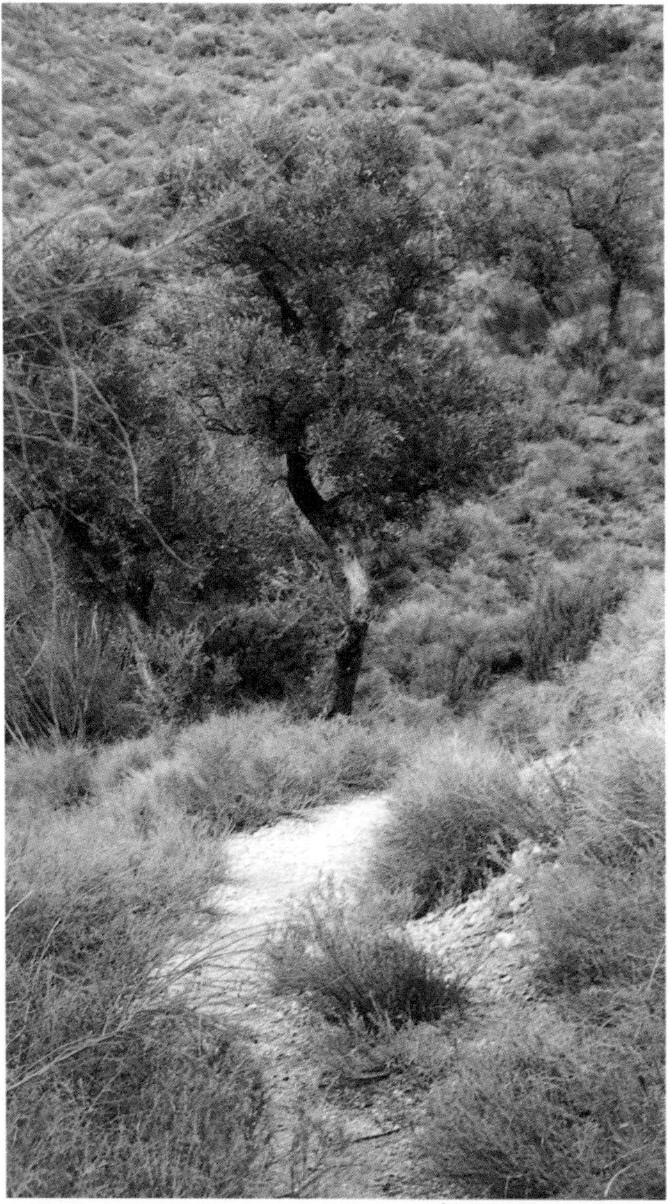

Distance:	12 km
Time Required:	6.5/7 hours
Rating:	Medium/Difficult
Maps: 1:50000	Sierra Nevada General Map or Lanjarón (1042) and Berja (1043)

From Bérchules to Juviles

The Walk of the Berber Villages

This longish day walk follows a large loop of the GR7, the long-distance path that crosses the southern flank of the Sierra Nevada. It is an astonishingly varied walk and you visit no fewer than five villages along the way. Although there is one slightly dull stretch when you pass beneath Cadiar, this walk is really special and some sections of the path are as pretty as any in the Alpujarras. But remember that between the River Guadalfeo and Juviles there is a difference in height of 450m (about 1500 feet) to negiotiate. If you are reasonably fit and get going early from Bérchules, you'll have ample time to picnic along the way and still be in Juviles in time to make the late afternoon bus back to your point of departure. Much of the walk is along muleteer tracks that cut up and down the sides of steep-sided *barrancos* (gorges). There are a few short sections of tarmac as you pass through the various villages.

The Route

The walk begins at the Hotel Bérchules at the bottom of the village.

Turn left out of the hotel and then right at the first junction and walk downhill past a large ham shop to the adjacent village of Alcútar. At the outskirts of

the village, branch right at a sign for *centro población*. The road bears right, passes a fountain and a church. At the end of this street called Calle Iglesia, fork left into Calle, then sharp left again into Calle Real and continue downhill.

At house no.30, bear right and then again to the

left and continue down Calle Churre. Skirt round the bottom of the village until you reach a fountain where you branch right. You now pick up a beautiful path (cobbled in parts and called Camino del Río) that drops down through fig, almond and olive groves. Pass a water tank to the right of the path.

Eventually you reach a flatter area where you bear right, pass by a well-tended almond grove, and follow along the right bank of the river, which you shortly cross via a pretty stone bridge. On the other side of the river, the path bears right. Look for a sign for Narila. As you reach the outskirts of Narila **(35 mins)**, the track becomes a paved road.

Pass a fountain to your left, then cross a bridge with a metal-railing. Keep right and soon you reach the square in front of the church. Head across to the phone box, then drop down into a narrow alley that descends and reaches a pylon, where you bear

sharply right. The path zigzags back down towards the river, passing between two almond groves.

At the end of a breeze-block wall with a fence on top, the path turns left and follows a narrow path, running parallel to the river. Soon the path runs closer to the river and you come to a point where the banks are shored up on both sides. Here **(55 mins)** pick up a track (a causeway of sorts) and continue until you reach a fenced-off irrigation tank. Here turn left and continue on through the almond groves.

The path soon reaches the outskirts of Cadiar, where it bears slightly right and skirts round the bottom of the village (don't climb up towards the centre). Pass a fountain and soon a wooden sign for Lobras points your way. You reach a fork. The right option leads across the river, but you swing left on a track that hugs the river's left bank. This is the least attractive part of this circuit, but persevere.

The best of the walk is yet to come and there is astonishingly varied cultivation in the *huertas* or irrigated allotments of this flat river valley. Carry on past the football pitch to an ugly concrete bridge, where you cross to the right bank of the river Guadalfeo and pick up a track that at first hugs its right bank, passing between groves of olives and almonds.

The track becomes prettier. It cuts slightly away from the river. Look for red and white 'GR' waymarking. Pass a ruined farm, just to the right of the track, then begin climbing steeply up a much narrower path. Cross an *acequia*, descend, and then swing sharp right and climb steeply up Loma de San Agustín. Soon you come to another *barranco,* where the path bears right.

The countryside opens out and there are great views across to the Contraviesa Sierra. Pass over the top of a ridge **(2hrs)** and up ahead you will now see Lobras. The path drops down the left side of the Barranco de Albayar, passing through a fig and then an olive grove and eventually reaches the (dry) river.

Bear left along the river bed for about 100 yards to a marker post, where you swing right away from the river and wind up a steep path towards Lobras. It is cobbled in parts. Pass through olive groves. Any where round here would make a good picnic spot.

After more climbing, the path levels and meets a tarmac road, where you turn right and enter Lobras. The road divides and here you branch left into the village. At the church, bear left, descend, and then turn right past the *consultorio*. You meet the tarmac road once again. Turn left, pass the Villa Rodríguez Martín and, opposite the village's water tank **(2hrs 35 mins)**, bear left at a sign for Timar.

Careful! Just past the village rubbish tip (watch

for a marker post), bear right onto a path that runs along beside a water channel. You reach a (dry) stream. Follow its right bank for some 20 metres, then cross and continue to climb. The Barranco de Lobras is down to your left.

The landscape becomes more barren and there are lots of agave cactii. At the next fork go left and zigzag steeply up. Your path merges with a track that leads on up to the top of the pass, where you should be able to spot a marker post as you approach. As you come through this narrow breach in the mountainside, bear sharp right onto a well-defined track and, at the next fork, turn right again. The path descends for a short distance and then climbs steeply up once again through the terraces beneath Timar. Head towards a water tank, first crossing an irrigation channel and then a beautiful old threshing circle. After passing a ruin to your left, pick up a track that bears right, then passes the town cemetery before reaching the village (**3 hrs**).

The track comes in to meet a paved road. Stay on the same track. It runs just below the paved road and passes by a tiny chapel. Skirt round the bottom of the village and, just past the church, branch left. A green-posted fence runs to your right. Just past a lone cypress tree, bear left and then branch steep right at a marker post. There is a sign for Juviles.

You will be climbing up past several prickly-pear plants with a wall and a fence running to your left. Where they end, bear sharp left and look for another marker post. The path continues climbing, very steeply. There are spectacular rock strata over to your right. At the top of the pass, go through a gap in the rocks. On the other side of this pass, bear left. You now have the upper reaches of the Barranco de Lobras down to your right.

Soon the path climbs again, rather looser-surfaced and trickier because of erosion. To the left of the path, pick up an irrigation channel that you soon will cross. The path levels before descending and crossing the stream beneath Juviles. You now have a final steep haul up into the village, first along a cobbled path and then by track.

You arrive at a *chacinería*, where you bear right up the hill and meet the road to Bérchules. Turn left. Just along on the right hand side is the bus stop, next to the phone box . Treat yourself to a beer and a tapa in Bar Alonso (**4hrs**) before taking the bus. Or arrange a rendez-vous at Bar Alonso should you decide to return by taxi.

CAZORLA

The area.

The Cazorla Natural Park (the Parque Natural de las Sierras de Cazorla, Segura and Las Villas, to give it its full title) lies at the eastern edge of the province of Jaén and is about a two-hour drive north-east from Granada. The most common way to approach the Park is from the west by way of endless groves of olives that stretch away as far as the eye can see. After this unremitting monoculture, it comes as welcome relief to see, ahead in the distance, the jagged outline of the Peña de los Halcones rising up above the town of Cazorla (886m), the gateway to the Natural Park of the same name.

The Park is Spain's largest protected area and covers no less than 214,000 hectares of incredibly diverse terrain. There are vast extensions of pine forests, broad river valleys, deep canyons, spectacular waterfalls and jagged peaks of karst that rise to 2000 metres and more. You could not wish for more beautiful walking country.

The abundance of game on the thickly forested hillsides meant that the region was long popular as a place to hunt. But by the fifties, the pickings were becoming so scarce that the area was declared a National Hunting Reserve. The original idea was simple: to increase the number of moving targets. Red deer and wild boar were reintroduced, mouflon brought from France and fallow deer from the mountains of Segovia. Numbers were carefully monitored and hunting controlled, and it soon began to pay dividends. The population of the *cabra hispánica* (Spanish mountain goat) alone rose tenfold in less than two decades.

The subsequent declaration of the reserve as a Natural Park (1986), with far tighter controls on hunting, has helped make the region one of the very best in Spain for the observation of wild mammals. Add to this an impressive roll call of birds of prey (several types of eagle, griffon and egyptian vultures, goshawks, hobbies, etc.) and the exceptional flora (over 2000 species with no less than two dozen of them endemic to the Park), and you begin to get the measure of the Park.

Most walkers base themselves in Cazorla, at the south eastern tip of the Park. The area immediately to the east contains some of the Park's most dramatic scenery and, although the town attracts many visitors, it makes an ideal base for some of the walks described in this section. Without your own transport, the other walks listed here require more logistical planning and you'll need to rely on taxis or buses to get you up into the Park.

In recent years the number of agencies offering 4-Wheel drive ("ecological"!) excursions have multiplied and so, too, have the number of ugly tourist developments stretching along the Guadalquivir valley. But both Hornos and Segura, starting points for two of the walks at the northern end of the park, are well away from the more touristy bits, and either of these quiet mountain villages is well worth an overnight stay.

The best time to walk here is from late March to early June and from September to early November. Temperatures plummet in winter and roads are often closed with snow. To really enjoy the walks in the Park, you need to be in reasonably good shape. Nearly all of the itineraries described in this chapter have at least one long, steep climb. Try to avoid the weekends and public holidays in Cazorla.

Other Walks

Don't waste time with the Park Authorities Office in Cazorla. They have absolutely no written or even verbal advice to offer. And the tourist offices in Cazorla are really just private travel agencies that try to sell you one of their own, guided walks. The Penthalon guide *Andar por El Parque Natural de las Sierra de Cazorla, Segura y Las Villas* by Gonzalo Crespo lists (in Spanish) some routes in the Park (nearly all up and down walks) but most require a lengthy

drive first thing. At the northern end of the Park, a number
of routes have been waymarked out from the village of Siles.
It is an attractive area although rather less dramatic than
that around Cazorla. The Alpina 1.40000 series of maps (see
below) include a booklet describing (in Spanish) some walking routes. These are highlighted on the individual maps.

Maps.

The Pentathlon 1.50000 Plano Topográfico de las Sierras
de Cazorla, Segura y Las Villas, based on the IGN series
'L', covers the whole of the area in just one map but it is
rather unwieldy. Other good maps easily found in Cazorla
are the Alpina, 1.40000 series. If planning to do all of the
walks detailed in this chapter, you will need three maps.
Sierra de Cazorla, Sierra de Segura I and Sierra de Segura
II/Las Villas.

Best Places to Sleep

Cazorla

Molino la Farraga.

Tel: 953 721 249.

A beautiful converted mill just outside town. Unquestionably the nicest place to stay in Cazorla. Approx. 60 euros. (Taxis: Urbano 953 72 17 33 or Antonio 953 72 08 37). **Best eats:** here or at Restaurante La Cueva de Juan Pedro, just 2 minutes away.

Hostal Guadalquivir.

Tel: 953 720 268.

A friendly, family-run hostal close to Cazorla's main square and popular with walking groups from the UK. Rooms are basic, but clean. 40 euros. (Taxis: see above). **Best Eats**. La Cueva de Juan Pedro.

La Finca Mercedes.

Tel: 953 721 087.

Just outside Cazorla, on the road to La Iruela. The rooms are excellent, with views, and both food and rooms are excellent value. Pool and garden. 35 euros. (Taxis: Urbano 953 72 17 33 or Antonio 953 72 08 37). **Best Eats**: here or at Bar La Cueva de Juan Pedro in town.

Parador El Adelantado.

Tel: 953 727 075
Fax: 953 721 075.

The best thing about this place is its beautiful, isolated position just beyond El Puerto del Tejo on the other side of the high ridge above Cazorla. But it is a long drive from the town (40+ minutes). 80–95 euros. (Taxis: see above). **Best Eats:** here.

Segura de la Sierra

El Mirador de Messía de Leiva.

Tel: 953 482 101.

Beautifully decorated apartments at the heart of this pretty village that has an attractive restaurant offering regional specialities. 55 euros. (Taxis: nearest in Orcera (7km away), Sr Herrero 953 48 21 12). **Best Eats:** here.

Hornos de Segura

Apartamentos Reiza.

Tel: 953 495 106.

Small apartments for two to six persons at the edge of the village, recently opened with all the trimmings. 45–50 euros. (Taxi: Angel 953 49 50 71). **Best Eats**. Restaurante Reiza in village centre, two minutes away.

Hotel de Montaña Los Parrales.

Tel: 953 126 170

A small hotel, between Cazorla and Hornos/Segura, in a peaceful location over-looking the El Tranco reservoir. Pleasant rooms, simple home cooking, rather chaotic service. 35 euros including breakfast. (Taxis: see Cazorla). **Best Eats**. here.

Cazorla Circuit (short)

Distance.	5.5 km
Time Required.	2 hours
Rating.	Easy

Maps.
Alpina 1.40000 map. Sierra de Cazorla. or Penthalon 1.50000 Plano Topográfico de las Sierras de Cazorla, Segura y Las Villas

The Walk of Glenn's Mill

This is a short, easy walk out from Cazorla that covers little distance but gives you a feel for the valley and the kind of terrain that awaits you should you choose to do some of the longer circuits in the Park. It leaves the village from the beautiful Plaza de Santa María, then follows a dirt track gently up Cazorla's river valley before looping back to the village along a higher path. I can never walk this valley without fondly remembering Glenn Minard, an amiable American, who lived for many years in one of the old mills that you pass by on this walk. He chose a heavenly spot to spend the later years of his life.

The Route

The walk begins in front of the hotel Cuidad de Cazorla in the main square of Cazorla, the Plaza de la Corredera.

Cross the square and go down the street next to the Banesto bank. At the end of this street, bear left following signs for *Ruinas de Santa María*. Pass by a fountain and emerge into the square of Santa María. Cross the square, pass in front of the hostal/restaurante La Cueva and follow the street up passing by the ruined church of Santa María to your left.

Climb gradually upwards and, at the first fork, bear left into Camino del Angel. The paved road soon becomes a track and you cross the bridge over the river.

Pass by the Molino de la Farraga just to one side of the track and continue to

climb on a narrow path that soon meets with a track. Here go right and head up a narrow track that follows the left bank of the river.

The paved section of track comes to an end and here there is a sign for Cazorla 2.5 km (**30 mins**).

Here you swing hard round to the left and climb up a dirt road passing a small shed built into the rocks. The track comes up to an attractive house with a wooden terrace where it swings right into a grove of olives and then bears round to the left again. You are now heading uphill towards a large cairn.

You reach a parking space beside another pretty house. Here swing left and zigzag up through the olive groves on a narrow footpath.

Soon you reach a better-surfaced footpath. Turn left onto this path and head back towards Cazorla. The river valley is down to your left and there are wonderful views down and across the valley.

You pass a water deposit on your right and the path begins to descend. You soon pass by a second water deposit and, just before reaching the first of the town's buildings, bear sharp left and drop down to meet Calle Paseo del Solar.

Continue steeply on down, pass by bar Torrecillas to your left and then swing left into Calle del Solar Bajo.

Continue down some steep steps and at the botttom turn right into Calle de la Torre. At the end of this street, bear left and then right into Calle de Mariano Estremera.

Turn left at the end of the street and then sharp right and follow this street along past the Agencia de la Seguridad Social. Turn left at the end, descend and then bear right into Calle Gomes Calderón. You arrive back at the Plaza de la Corredera (**1hr 30 mins**).

Cazorla Circuit (Long)

Distance	16 km or 12 km (see below)
Time Required.	7/7.5 hours or 6/6.5 hrs
Rating.	Med/Difficult or Medium

Maps.
Alpina 1.40000 map. Sierra de Cazorla. or Penthalon 1.50000 Plano Topográfico de las Sierras de Cazorla, Segura y Las Villas

The Walk of the High Sierra

This circular walk from Cazorla, mostly along high mountain trails, is one of the Sierra's classic itineraries and well deserves its reputation. A long climb of nearly 900m up from the village takes you to a high pass from where the peak of El Gilillo (1848m) is easily climbed. The views on a clear day of the distant Sierra Nevada alone make this walk worth the effort. From the Gilillo pass, a beautiful high mountain trail brings you back to Cazorla in a long, lazy loop – a wonderful reward for your efforts earlier in the day. If you find the long climb intimidating and wish to avoid the initial 3 km or so of mountain road above Cazorla (there are very few vehicles and the views are wonderful), you could take a taxi to the barrier by the Hotel Ríogazas (see easier option below). It is important to be prepared for cold conditions on the higher, often windy section of this walk. If climbing Gilillo, add an hour to the timings below.

The Route

The walk begins in in front of the hotel Cuidad de Cazorla in the main square of Cazorla, the Plaza de la Corredera.

Turn left along the top of the square and take the first left up Calle del Carmen. Climb steeply and opposite a church turn right into Calle Mercedes Gómez. Pass the *juzgados* and at the end of the road swing left, climb, and then bear sharp left again into Calle del Herrón. Follow this street up. It bears left, then right and then narrows to become a path that climbs past the last of the village's houses.

Bear left at a water tank and head up through the pines (following white and red waymarking) to a viewing platform where you meet with the track that runs all the way round the bowl of the valley **(25mins)**.

Turn right onto the track. Soon you'll have good views of Cazorla down to the right. Ignore a waymarked GR cross telling you are on the wrong route. On the other side of the valley, the Castillo de Cinco Esquinas (the five cornered castle) is clearly visible on its rather bare, hill-top perch. Continue round the bowl of the valley and cross the Ríogazas River, still keeping to main track. Pass a spring to your left and soon you will arrive at a white hut with a stop sign/barrier **(1 hr 5 mins)**.

Traffic into the park is controlled during the summer months. Just down to your right is the hotel Riogazas. Careful! Continue past the barrier for just 60 metres to a sign to the left of the track (for Ríogazas). Here swing sharp left off the track and climb. At first the path is indistinct but after just a few yards it improves.

You wind up through the pines and meet the track again. Go straight over and continue on up the path. Soon you meet the track a second time at a point where there is a large sign with a map of the park. It is confusing – the arrow marking your position is in the wrong place!

Cross the track and pick up the path once again, just behind this sign. Zigzagging up, you soon reach more open terrain and the path divides by a cairn. Turn left and climb on up into the pine forest. You meet with a cliff face where you cross a rock-fall and then descend slightly before bearing sharply right and climbing again. Cairns mark the path at this point.

To your right, on a clear day, you can see the distant Sierra Nevada and, a few kilometers distant, the plateau of El Chorro. The vegetation becomes sparser and the path rather looser underfoot as you climb on to the top of the 1740m Puerto Gilillo pass **(2 hrs 30 mins)**.

Here you could bear off to the right and climb Gilillo (1848m). The trig point at the top is clearly visible from here. Allow 45 minutes to get up and down. Otherwise, go down on the other side of the pass for just 20 yards and turn left towards a mountain refuge.

Just above it, you pick up a narrow footpath that runs along beneath the ridge of the Loma de Castellones. At times it is indistinct but there are cairns to guide you. The path climbs and crosses the ridge that has been running along to your right at its far end **(3 hrs)**.

Soon a path comes in to meet yours from the right. You stick to your same path and shortly pass through a stand of pine and juniper. Pass by two large cairns to the left of

the path. After descending for a short distance, you climb again along a beautiful section of path. At a large cairn the path swings right and descends again then, after meeting another stand of pines, emerges into a more open area.

Follow cairns across this flatter area. There is a jagged line of limestone jutting vertically upwards. This would be a beautiful picnic spot. A green arrow on one of the rocks indicates the course you should follow. At the end of this flat area, the path descends slightly, bears left and soon you can see the red roof of the Parador de Turismo down to your right.

You reach El Puerto del Tejo and the path divides. One path swings right to the Parador but you turn left, following a green arrow. The path contours round the mountainside. You see the occasional red dot as waymarking. Soon you drop more steeply downwards and pass beneath some power lines. The path leads you to the abandoned farm of Prado Redondo **(4 hrs 20 mins)**.

Just metres before you reach the farm, swing left, descend a few yards and then swing left again along the bottom of the farm's threshing circle, now on your left. Pick up a path that climbs into the pine forest, at first rather indistinctly but it soon improves and you will see cairns.

Leaving some tumble-down pens to your left, the path bears right and waymarking reappears (white and red GR bands). After passing through more pines, the landscape again opens out and you head towards a pylon, picking up a (dry) water course. Once you have passed this pylon, you'll soon see the castle above La Iruela down beneath you.

A final steep and stony section brings you to the Ermita de La Virgen de la Cabeza where you head for

the wooden cross just to the left of the chapel and pick up a steep path that drops down onto a track. It runs down to meet the track that you followed along towards the barrier at the start of the walk. Cross the track to the 'mirador', bear sharp right and follow a path back down to the outskirts of Cazorla and from here retrace your footsteps back down to the main square **(5 hrs 30 mins)**.

Distance.	9 km or 15 km (see below)
Time Required.	4/4.5 or 6.5/7 hours
Rating.	Med or Medium/Difficult (long

Maps.
Alpina 1.40000 map. Sierra de Cazorla.
or Penthalon 1.50000 Plano Topográfico de
las Sierras de Cazorla, Segura y Las Villas

The Walk
of the Thirsty Bear

This tremendously varied walk makes for a great full day's
excursion. The first section is a longish up-and-down loop
through pine forest with views of some of the park's most
spectacular, craggy peaks. You later follow a wonderful
mountain trail that cuts up from the Guadalquivir valley
through a high pass before it winds its way down and around
the Escribano peak to Cazorla. The path has wonderful views
up the Guadalquivir Valley and out across the sea of olive
groves that stretches west from Cazorla. Unlike most walks
in this book, you need transport to the beginning of the walk.
But don't give the taxi fare a second thought. The ride up
into the park is alone memorable enough to justify the ex-
pense. You can easily make this into a shorter walk by beginning at El Puente de las Herrerias instead of in Vadillo
Castril, thus cutting out the steep loop through the pine
forest. If you do the whole route you have two steep climbs,
one of almost 300m first thing and then the second longer
climb of almost 400m up and past the Fuente del Oso.

The Long Route.

The walk begins at the
entrance of the village of
Vadillo Castril as you come
from Cazorla.

Head along Calle
Cabañas towards Café Bar
Leñador and then turn left
into Calle Gualay. At the
end of the street, turn right
and drop down onto a dirt
track and cross the river
via a concrete footbridge.
Swing right and you come
to the road that you follow
to a point just before the
bridge over the Barranco
de la Sarga.

Here swing left onto a track that cuts away from the road, bears right, crosses a stream bed and then climbs. You meet with a broader track. Here bear left and continue climbing through the pines. The path divides and you bear right. It then divides again. Take the left hand option and continue to zigzag upwards. The views improve. You reach a clearing in the pines where another track comes in from the right. You continue on the same course and soon you will arrive at a fenced-off area **(45 mins)**.

Pick up an indistinct path that runs up just to the right of the fence and then meets with a tarmac road. Turn right onto the road and – careful! - follow it along for just a few hundred yards and then turn off to the right onto a sandy track. It may have a chain across it.

You now begin to wind gently down between the pines. there are impressive views out to the jagged peaks of the Loma de la

Mesa and Rastrillo de la Víbora (1635m). The track loops round the top of a stream and passes by the ruins of a *cortijo* or farm **(1 hr 10 mins)**. This could be a pretty spot for a first break.

Leaving the farm, continue on past some cypress trees and after about 100 metres, the track divides. Fork right and descend. You will have a (dry) stream to your right. Cross a rock fall and the path, sandy now, swings close to a rock face then crosses a (dry) stream. Here you bear right and continue dropping down, at first with the rock face close to your left. You cross a second rock fall and the path climbs slightly. The riverbed is still down to your right.

Soon the path zigzags down and takes up a lower course. You cross a (dry) stream, bear right and then the path comes back to the cliff face before reverting once again to track. Carry on down and soon another better defined track comes in from the right. Here go left and then almost immediately right and continue on down. Look for green arrows and the occasional cairn.

The path meets with the road at El Puente de la Herrerias **(2 hrs)**. Continue on as below.

Short Route

This short version starts at El Puente de las Herrerias.

Coming from Valdillo, cross the bridge and turn immediately right down towards a bar. Cross a small bridge and pick up a path that heads up the hill from just behind a spring, to the left of the bar. Zigzag up the right hand side of the stream and reach a fork where you take the right hand option.

The path becomes wider and sandier and shortly you come to a marker post where you have three choices. Go directly across onto the middle path that swings right and continues to climb, fairly gently, up to the group of forestry commission buildings of La Fuente del Oso (The Bear's Spring). Climb up past the buildings to the road **(30 mins)**.

At the road, turn right, cross over the bridge and – careful! – swing immediately left across an open space and then bear right onto a path that climbs up through the pines. At first you follow a line of pylons upwards. Over to your left is the Cerro de la Torquilla.

When you come to a fork, don't turn right (this path descends towards the road) but rather branch left and climb up through the pine forest towards El Collado del Oso. This is a stunning section of path and is very easy to follow. Soon there are marvellous views up the Guadalquivir valley, over to your right. Eventually you pass through El Puerto de los Arenales (1358m) **(45 mins)**. This would be a good picnic spot.

The panorama now completely changes. You are looking out across the endless olive groves that lie to the east of Cazorla.

The path winds steeply down through the pines on the eastern side of the pass. There is waymarking. The forest opens out and the path bears right and passes to the right of a small building.

The path continues to contour round the Escribano mountain and shortly the Templar's Castle of La Iruela comes into sight. After descending steeply down, the path drops to cross a (dry) streambed and – careful! - on a rock you'll see a red arrow pointing upwards **(2 hrs 15 mins)**.

Here swing right off the main path (a red GR cross suggests that you are going the wrong way but ignore it) and continue your descent.

As you approach the castle, keep close to the cliff on your left and follow a narrow path down that meets with the road by the swimming pool.

The last 20 metres are steep and loose. Turn left onto the road, pass beneath the castle (it is well worth a visit), then branch left again and head through the centre of the village. At the far end of the village, go straight across the road that leads from La Iruela to the Ermita de la Virgen de la Cabeza and drop steeply down to return to the square at the north end of Cazorla **(3 hrs)**.

The Río Borosa

The Walk of the deep Gorge and the high Waterfalls

Distance.	19 km
Time Required.	7/7.5 hours
Rating.	Medium/Difficult

Maps.
Alpina 1.40000 map. Sierra de Cazorla.
or Penthalon 1.50000 Plano Topográfico de
las Sierras de Cazorla, Segura y Las Villas

The Sierra's best-known walk takes you along a beautiful section of the spectacular gorge of the Rio Borosa. It is a walk that seems to get better and better the higher you climb. After a stretch of forestry track, the gorge narrows down and you follow a spectacular wooden walkway suspended above the river. Later the gorge again opens out again and you come to a huge, natural ampitheatre of soaring limestone crags. From here, a steep climb takes you up to a high reservoir that you reach by following the course of a mill race that has been tunneled out of the mountainside. Don't worry if you think this route might be too long. You return by the same path, so the walk can be as far up-and-down as you like. But remember that you have a climb of 600m should you do the whole lot. Because this is such a well-known walk, it is best done on a weekday, out of the holiday season. Take a torch for the high sections of tunnel and in the warmer months remember your bathing costume. There are lovely river pools for swimming. The upper section of the walk is sometimes impassable in winter, so check with the Park rangers at Torre de Vinagre or with one of the agencies in Cazorla.

The Route

The walk begins from the car park on the left hand side of the road just before the trout farm (*piscifactoría*) of the río Borosa. (If arriving by car turn off the A 319 by the Centro de Interpretación Torre del Vinagre and follow signs for the Central Eléctrica).

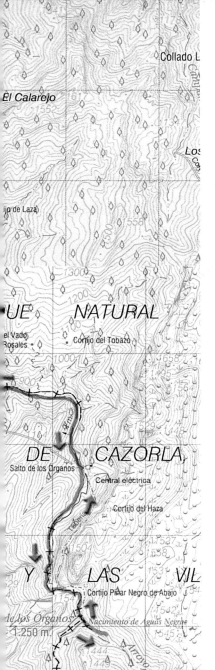

Cross the river and leave your car in the park to the left of the road just before the *piscifactoría*. Walk past the fish farm, cross a bridge, then turn right and follow a track along the left bank of the river. Pass a *zona de baño* – a great spot for a swim on your return - and shortly afterwards a fishing reserve called *acotado de pesca sin muerte*. (So if you manage to tickle out a trout, you must put it back).

Cross a concrete bridge, swing left along the river's right bank for a short distance and then cross back to the left bank via a wooden bridge. At a point where the track begins to bear left and climb, branch right on path marked Cerrada de Elias **(35 mins)**.

Now follow a pretty path along the left bank of the river. It crosses a foot-bridge and, after following the right bank of the Borosa along, crosses second bridge back to the left bank. The Borosa's gorge begins to narrow down. Soon you cross back over the river and follow a hanging cat-walk along above the river, through a truly beautiful stretch of the gorge.

The path drops down and meets with the track again. Continue on up the gorge, crossing back and forth over the river as the gorge, ever more spectacular, begins to open out. Up ahead the strata of La Cuerda de Las Banderillas and La Peña Plumera look like the layers of some fantastic wedding cake and, when the track bears slightly right, the towering massif of Castellón del Haza de Arriba(1504m) comes into sight.

Soon you see the pipeline that funnels the water down the left hand side of the valley to the generat-ing station (*el central eléctrica*). Cross over a bridge **(1 hr 45 mins)** and then follow a fence just to the right of the generating station and its various outbuildings.

Go past a spring, then cross a narrow wooden bridge and pick up a path at a sign pointing you towards Laguna de Valdeazores. The path climbs steeply up the left bank of the river. Steel yourself. You have a climb of some 300m ahead of you if you wish to follow the walk all the way.

Soon the path crosses over a stream. You could end the walk, or take a break, beside a rock pool that you soon see to your right. It is possible to scramble down. Otherwise continue climbing.

To the left of you is the Picón del Haza. For much of the year, a waterfall runs off its eastern flank. The path climbs up to the spectacular ampitheatre of the gorge's higher reaches. The mountains rise almost sheer up to 1500m. You now see red dots as waymarking. Soon you'll see another waterfall – El Salto de los Órganos –over to your right. The path swings steeply up over loose scree, then bears right. At a point where you see another waterfall and the remains of a dam, the path swings sharply to the left and then climbs steeply up towards an electricity pylon. Before you reach the pylon bear right and continue up to a sign for Nacimiento de Aguas Negras and Laguna de Valdeazores.

The path leads you into the tunnel cut to bring water to the mill race. It is almost 350 m long! Pass through a second tunnel and look for a dam up ahead and beyond it a reservoir – El embalse del Borosa, La Laguna de Aguas Negras or el Embalse de los Órganos, depending on the map you happen to have (**2 hrs 45mins**).

Here the path divides and you bear left. (You could bear right, cross to the right hand side of the reservoir, then continue for a quarter of an hour to the beautiful Laguna de Valdeazores. But because many 4-wheel drive excursions head for this spot, I recommend the option described opposite).

Climb away from the water course along the left hand side of the reservoir, then climb up the valley of the Arroyo del Infierno to the Nacimiento de Aguas Negras (**3 hrs**) where the Rio Borosa rises from beneath the rocks. This would be a great place to lunch or have elevenses if you started out early.

You now retrace your footsteps all the way back down the gorge to arrive back at your point of departure (**5 hrs 30 mins**).

Segura
de la Sierra Circuit

Distance.	11 km
Time Required.	4/4.5 hours
Rating.	Medium

Maps.
Alpina 1.40000 map. Sierra de Segura I.
or Penthalon 1.50000 Plano Topográfico de
las Sierras de Cazorla, Segura y Las Villas

The Walk
of the Hidden Terraces

This walk has superb views of the different mountain ranges
that surround Segura and makes for an interesting half-
day excursion. After contouring round Fuentecicas, you have
a short section of very quiet road to negotiate before returning to forestry track. You later drop down into the valley of
the Arroyo de los Corazones before climbing almost 250m
back up to Segura via a steep, narrow and spectacular footpath. This path takes you past a series of fertile terraces
that have been spectacularly sculpted out of the steep
mountainside. This is the most beautiful part of the walk
and would be a good place to break for a picnic.

The Route

The walk begins in the
Plaza de la Encomienda,
the small square in the
centre of the village,
opposite the church of
Nuestra Señora del
Collado.

Facing the church, turn
right, pass Bar Peralta,
and descend gently. After
passing a fountain to your
right, leave the last houses
of the village behind. Pass
a row of cypress trees to
your left and just past the
municipal swimming pool
bear left onto a track that
leads down to the old
washhouse.

At the very first fork,
swing right onto a sandy
track and climb up through
the pine trees. You are
contouring round the
western flank of the
Picoputas peak. There are
wonderful views across the
valley of the River Orcera
to the peak of Peñalta
(1412m), easily spotted

because of the fire observation hut at its peak.

Climbing gently upwards,
you soon reach an area of
more recent pine planta-
tion. A track comes in from
the right to merge with
yours. Carry straight on
and soon you pass by a goat
farm, Hoya Chaspinar, to
your right **(30 mins)**.

Shortly after the farm, the
track swings round to the
right and descends through
the pines. The peak of
Fuentecicas towers above
you to your right and,
looking left, you have fine
views across the valley to
Navalperal. Pass a spring,
la Fuente de la Tejadilla.
The track now climbs gently
upwards and you arrive at
the tarmac road **(1 hr)**.

Swing left onto the road
(there is very little traffic)
and, after just 800m, turn
right at a sign for
Moralejos. The castle above
Segura soon comes into
view. You reach a ridge
with a line of electricity
pylons at a point where the
road loops sharply left.
Here swing right off the

road onto a track leading
down towards a pylon. The
Trújula gorge is down to
your left. After following
the ridge along, the path
soon drops very steeply
downwards. Segura is
again visible from here.
The track bears round to
the right and contours
round the Collado del
Acebuche, then narrows to
become a path **(1 hr 45
mins)** that continues to
drop down through pines.

You reach an olive grove
(a good spot for a picnic).
The narrow path loops
down and crosses the
Arroyo de los Corazones,
then zigzags up the other
side and meets with a
track. Turn left here and go
down the hill, parallel to
the (dry) stream. You come
to an area where a bull-
dozer has been at work.
Don't take the path that
crosses the river but rather
carry on down the right
bank of the stream along a
narrow path that soon
leads you past an over-
hanging rock-face.

Careful! Just 200 yards
after this rock face you

must swing right onto a very narrow path (look for a cairn) that leads you up the side of the gorge. It swings behind a lonesome olive tree and climbs.

At a first fork, keep right, continue on upwards and soon you pass by stands of prickly pears and agave. Winding on up, you meet another narrow path. Swing right here and continue climbing, now through an olive grove.

You reach a flatter area where the path runs between huge agave cactii and then climbs again steeply. You reach a fenced-off area of fertile terracing where the path meets with a water channel. Bear sharp right here and carry on up. You will now have a fence to your left. The path zigzags away from the terracing and continues to climb steeply upwards and then runs into a track **(2 hrs 30 mins)**

Continue on up. Soon the track swings hard right and in front you will again see the castle of Segura. The track leads on past an extraordinarily ugly breeze block enclosure to your right and then levels, passes an abandoned *cortijo* and reaches the road, just beyond the architectural anarchy of Finca Galiano. Here you swing left onto the road you follow back to your point of departure **(3 hrs)**.

Distance.	15 km
Time Required	3.5/4 hours
Rating.	Easy

Maps.
Alpina 1.40000 map. Sierra de Cazorla.
or Penthalon 1.50000 Plano Topográfico de
las Sierras de Cazorla, Segura y Las Villas

The Walk
of the Olive Groves

The terrain around Hornos de Segura is rather less rugged
than that you encounter on the walks around Cazorla and,
because access is more difficult, it attracts far fewer visitors. But the walking here is memorable and this walk gives
you a good feel for the area. Much of it leads leads through
olive groves and pine plantations and there are beautiful
views out across the El Tranco reservoir. This easy half-day
excursion involves little climbing and most of it takes you
along dirt tracks where you can admire the scenery and not
worry about where your feet are going. There is also a short
section of tarmac road but there is very little traffic. Holly
oaks have invaded sections of the path near the beginning
of the walk, so you may prefer to wear long trousers.

The Route

The walk begins in Hornos
de Segura at Bar El Cruce,
easily spotted as you arrive
in the village.

From here cross the road
past a bus stop and bear
right up the road leading to
Pontones. Pass a large
building to the left and
then turn left off the road.
Passing just to the left of a
grey garage door, you pick

up a dirt track that climbs
gradually up through
groves of olives and al-
monds that shortly give
way to plantations of pine.
The path divides (**10
mins**).

Bear right and, after just
ten metres at a second
fork, again bear right. The
track ends and becomes a
path that runs along the
bottom of an olive grove.
Look for red crosses to

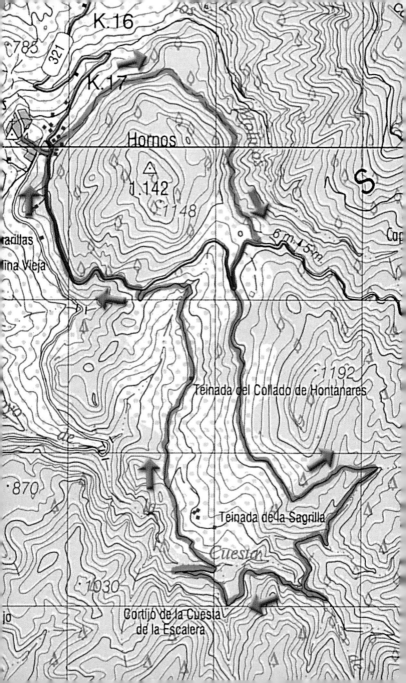

guide you at this stage. Although slightly over-grown this is a beautiful section of path. Over to your left is the rugged peak of Los Ranchales (1513 m) and beneath you to the left is the gorge of Arroyo los Molinos. The path forks **(20 mins)**.

Keep right here and continue on through the pines. Soon you join a wider track where you bear right and then climb for a short distance up to an olive grove. Here swing left and down and you'll pick up a track that continues on the same course. It enters another stand of pines and continues to climb.

The track now meets with the Hornos- Pontones road. Turn right here and continue for 700 metres and, at a hairpin bend where the road bears sharply round to the right, turn left onto a track that leads you past an enor-mous rock **(55 mins)**.

You will see various tracks branching off into the olive groves but you keep to the main track. The path divides at a point where three large rocks have been piled up. Here bear sharp left. Above you to the left is the Cerro del Caballete. Ignore a turning where there is a sign for the farm of Hontanares. You reach a line of pylons where you swing left.

Soon you bear sharply right again and begin to descend quite steeply, following a tributary of the Arroyo de la Cuesta de la Escalera downhill. In this area, you will see a number of pines that have been snapped off at the base, the result of heavy snowfall. You reach a junction. One track swings left up the hill but you keep to the right and loop down to the Arroyo de la Cuesta de la Escalera, where there is a small dam across the river.

Don't try crossing here. Keep to the track and, after 200 metres, loop sharp right, descend and cross a bridge over the stream. Bearing round to the right, you soon pass by

Now pick up a better track that winds up through the olive groves. Up above you to your right, you'll soon see the farm of Tiná de la Sagrilla. The path divides.

Take the lefthand fork and descend towards a group of pine trees and carry on past a chain that crosses the track. It will tell you that you have been walking across private land but don't worry, the sign is to discourage wild asparagus pickers. You have been following a public right-of-way.

the abandoned Cortijo de la Cuesta de la Escalera, a good spot to break for a picnic. You cross a (dry) stream bed and shortly afterwards the track hairpins to the right (don't continue straight on) and soon you cross the (dry) stream once again. There are stepping stones **(2 hrs 10 mins)**.

Follow the track up through the olive groves. Pass a ruin on your left, then a water tank, and continue to climb gradually up until you again reach the Hornos-Pontones road. Turn left and follow the road back to the village. Although you are now on a tarmac road, there is virtually no traffic and you have wonderful views out across the Embalse del Tranco. After passing a mirador you arrive back in the village **(3 hrs)**.

Feedback from readers about changes to any of the routes in this guide and suggestions for new routes are most welcome, and will be used in the next edition. Senders of the 10 most useful letters will receive a free copy of the next edition. Please write to Guy Hunter-Watts, El Tejar, 29430 Montecorto (Málaga) or email me at eltejar@mercuryin.es

Many thanks.

acequia – a man-made irrigation channel. Many of those in Andalucía date from the Moorish period

alcornoques – cork oaks

almiñar – a minaret

arroyo – a stream

ayuntamiento – town hall

barranco – the steep, shaley gorges that so typify the Alpujarras

cairn – small pile of rocks/stones serving as way-marker

calera – a pit where lime was made by firing limestone.

canuto – a steep sided gorge where a warm, humid climate has fostered a surprisingly diverse vegetation

capilla – a chapel

cerro – a peak or mountain

choza – a simple hut or dwelling, often with a thatched roof

cortijo – a farm – from a few to several thousand acres large

coto (de caza) – a hunting reserve

dehesa – an area of forest which has been partially cleared in order to leave selected species eg evergreen and cork oak. Livestock can graze on the more open ground and also benefit from the fruits eg acorns for the pigs.

era – a threshing area, often circular

guiri – a foreigner (slang)

G.R. – short for 'Gran Recorrido' or 'long distance footpath'

huerta – a small patch of cultivated land

humilladero – a small mountain shrine

karst – limestone

laja – a jagged ridge, formed when the limestone strata run vertically upwards, a typical feature of the Alcornocales Park.

mirador – a viewing point

puerto – a mountain pass

rejas – window grills

romería – a procession and picnic, often involving an open-air mass at a chapel or shrine at the outskirts of a village

sierra – a range of mountains

secadero – flat platforms used in the Cómpeta area for laying out grapes in the sunshine.

tinao – a roof spanning a village street in the Alpujarras

HOJA DE PEDIDO/*Order Form*

Atención de: ____________________
To:
Fax: ____________________

De Parte de: ____________________
From:
Fax: ____________________

Fecha: ____________________
Date:

Referente a/*Subject:*

Pedido de Mapas *Map Order*

Estimados Señores/Señoras,
Dear Sir/Madam,

Les ruego mandarme los siguientes mapas, contra reembolso:
Please send me the following maps, to be paid on receipt of order:

No(s) de Mapa(s):	*Map reference*(s):
________	____________________
________	____________________
________	____________________
________	____________________
________	____________________
________	____________________

Les ruego mandar el pedido en nombre de:
Please send order in the name of:

A esta dirección:
To this address: ____________________

____

____

____

____

Les agradezco su amble cooperación.
Many thanks for your help.

Aracena

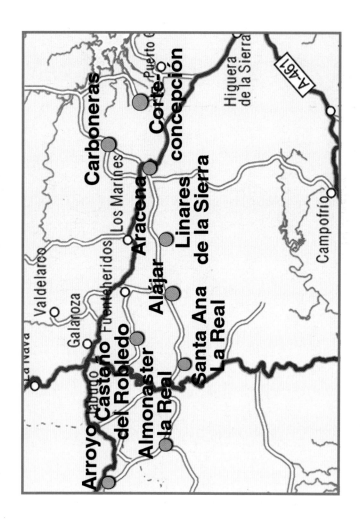

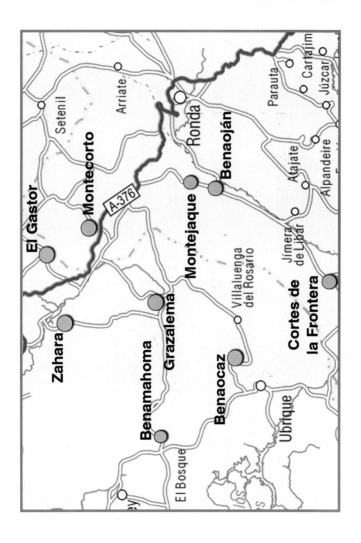

Los Alcornocales

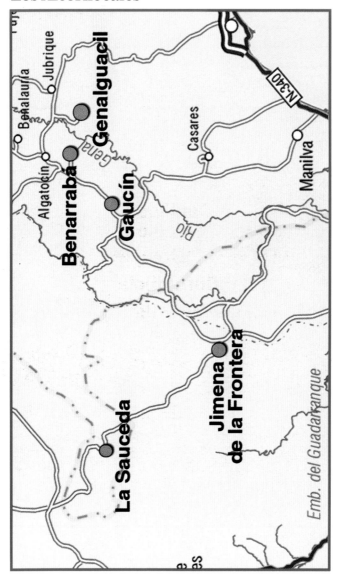

The Alpujarras

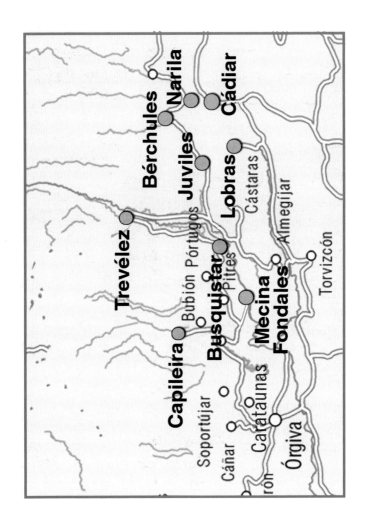

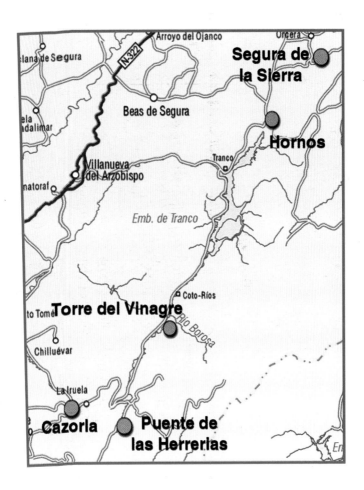

For a full list of our
essential books on Spain contact:

Santana Books
Apartado 422,
29640 Fuengirola, (Malaga), Spain

Tel: 952 485 838. Fax: (34) 952 485 367
E-mail: sales@santanabooks.com

UK Representatives
Aldington Books Ltd.,
Unit 3(b) Frith Business Centre,
Frith Road, Aldington,
Ashford, Kent TN25 7HJ.
Tel: 01233 720 123. Fax: 01233 721 272
E-mail: sales@aldingtonbooks.co.uk
www.aldingtonbooks.co.uk